POWER
cables

The Ultimate Guide to Knitting Inventive Cables

LILY M. CHIN

INTERWEAVE
interweavestore.com

Editor: Anne Merrow

Tech Editor: Therese Chynoweth

Model Photography: Joe Hancock

Photo Styling: Pam Chavez

Hair and Makeup: Kathy MacKay and Jill Vincent

Swatch Photography: Joe Coca

Illustrator: Ann Sabin Swanson

Cover and Interior Designer: Connie Poole

Production: Katherine Jackson

Interweave Press LLC
201 East Fourth Street
Loveland, CO 80537 USA
interweavestore.com

Printed in China by C&C Offset.

Library of Congress Cataloging-in-Publication Data

Chin, Lily M.
  Power cables : the ultimate guide to knitting inventive
cables / Lily M. Chin.
      p. cm.
  Includes bibliographical references and index.
  ISBN 978-1-59668-167-5
  1. Knitting--Patterns. 2. Sweaters. I. Title.
  TT825.C3934 2010
  746.43'20432--dc22

                      2009051646

10 9 8 7 6 5 4 3 2 1

dedication

This book is dedicated to my nieces and nephews: Victor, Janis, Michelle, and Ricky. Mostly, it is for my great-nephew Luke. You are all like my own children and represent that next generation. I love you all very much.

ACKNOWLEDGMENTS

Thanks to Tricia Waddell and Anne Merrow for their patience and understanding. Special thanks to my army of knitters: Dolly Maguire (Turnaround Shawl), Margarete Dahlke (Textured Tote), JoAnn Moss (Pinstriped Pullover), Bertha Falck (Five-way Shrug), Tom Jensen (Background Stitches Cable Vest), Jeanne Dowling (Honeycomb V-neck Pullover and Scarf), Claire Brenner (Socks), Leslie Kirk (Bi-Colored Brioche Stole), and Mary Lou Risley (Staghorn Coat). Of course, appreciation goes to the kind and generous yarn companies for their supplies contributions. Lots of kudos to Karabella Yarns, who provided Aurora 8 yarn for all the swatches shown. Tremendous appreciation to Barbara Hillery Van Elsen for always lending an ear. Lastly, all my love and consideration to my long-suffering husband, Clifford Pearson. I don't know anyone else who would put up with my perpetual inattention to him.

foreword

Lily's greatest single talent is her ability to take knitting to places it hasn't been before. And—lucky us!—she is happy to take knitters along for the ride. Those of us who accompany Lily on her knitting explorations are treated not only to the innovative designs that spring from her needles, but also to a thorough and patient explanation of the hows and whys of new techniques so that we can incorporate them into our own knitting. Some designers are content to scratch the surface of a topic and call it good; Lily delves as far into her subject matter as is humanly possible, twisting and turning it to see all the possible angles. And she wants to share her discoveries with the rest of us.

Power Cables will stretch the horizons of even the most experienced knitters. No longer is the humble rope cable content to sit quietly on the front of a sweater—now it demands to pirouette gloriously across knitted fabric, showing how beautiful it can be on every side. And who knew what interesting textures were hiding on the other side of plaits and braids? Lily allows these stitches and the knitters who knit them the freedom to do things they've never been able to do before. I can guarantee that once you've picked up Power Cables, you'll never look at cable stitches the same way again. What are you waiting for? Adventure awaits!

—Janet Szabo, author of The "I Hate to Finish Sweaters" Guide, Aran Sweater Design, and Cables, Volume 1: The Basics and publisher of "Twists and Turns: The Newsletter for Lovers of Cable Knitting"

contents

who doesn't like cables?

Cables are a perennial favorite of knitters. Not difficult to do, cables intrigue us with their intricate-looking textures.

But when you want to use them in, say, a scarf or shawl or afghan, the sad fact is that the back of a cable isn't very presentable. Well, no longer! With my very simple reversible cables, cables can look equally lovely from both sides. Once you understand the basics of cables, you can advance to more intriguing reversibles, such as two-color reversibles or cable patterns that produce different patterns on each side. You can even try out some phony or mock cables.

This book explores the possibilities of the knitted cable's form and function. Although cables of all kinds will be discussed, special attention will be given to three areas: my system for charting cables of all kinds (both regular and reversible); reversible cables; and integrating cables into a design, not just applying them.

This is not the only book on knitting cables, but I am a strong believer in empowerment. I want to give you, the reader, the tools to come up with your own cable patterns. I hold to that old adage: "Give a man a fish and he'll eat for a day. Teach a man to fish and he'll eat for a lifetime." (Actually, teach him to fish and he'll be in a boat all day drinking beer!)

It is also my desire to impart the ability to decipher complex-seeming cables. How often have you stood in line at the post office behind someone wearing an Aran sweater? Didn't you want to pull it apart to see how to re-create it? Not only will this book break down the anatomy of cables so that you will have a clear, basic understanding of cables, it will also teach you to look at an existing pattern and figure out how it's done. You will be able to design and knit your own original, never-before-seen cable patterns.

It has been over twenty years since I embarked upon my quest for reversible cables, and it has become synonymous with my name. It has been the subject of some of my most popular classes since 1990. *Power Cables* covers a comprehensive potpourri of all methods. It's amazing how a simple technique can keep one in stitches (and myself in business) for over twenty years!

how to use this book

Power Cables is full of techniques, stitch patterns, projects, and ideas to explore. To find what you need easily, here's how to use and identify the different parts.

The first **chapters** each explore a particular cable technique. Beginning with a fundamental understanding of basic cables, the techniques generally build on the previous chapters. Even if you have worked with cables before, don't skip Chapter 1: Understanding Cables, because it includes a new charting system just for cables! This revolutionary method will change the way you look at, plan, and knit cables.

Within each chapter, a number of **stitch files** show swatches that give you an opportunity to practice the techniques—but you can also use them like a stitch dictionary. A swatch in each Stitch File shows what the written pattern or chart looks like. Once the technique is familiar, tweak the Stitch File patterns to meet your knitting needs.

At the end of each chapter, **patterns** using the new techniques offer a great way to practice your skills while knitting beautiful wearable clothes and accessories.

At the end of the book comes Chapter 9: Cable Integration, which offers ways to design with cables. Use everything you've learned in *Power Cables* to start making your own cable knitting designs!

understanding
cables

What's a cable? A cable by any other name is usually comprised of a few stitches crossing over one another and changing positions. That is, the stitches are not worked "in order." For example, if a cable pattern is to be worked over the next 4 stitches, instead of working 1, 2, 3, 4, we might work 3, 4, then 1, 2. All of these stitches are usually worked in stockinette stitch (knit on the right side, purl on the wrong side). But even though cables are really composed of nothing but stitches worked out of order, an infinite number of combinations are at your fingertips.

BASIC CABLE PRIMER

There are only two kinds of cables: left and right. The directions are read from the bottom of the cable to the top in the direction of the knitting (**Fig. 1**). They are achieved by moving the stitches on the cable needle to either the back or the front. When changing positions, the first set of stitches (the ones originally closer to the tip of the left needle that are moved to a temporary holding position on the cable needle) cross over to the left, either from on top (or in front) of the next set of stitches or beneath (or behind) them.

When the first set of stitches crosses over on top of the next set of stitches, what you see from the front is the first set of stitches slanting to the left—a left cross. The stitches behind this left cross are not in full view from the front, but they slant to the right. When the first set of stitches crosses below the next set of stitches, this latter set of stitches winds up on the top, slanting to the right—a right cross. The first or bottom set of stitches is not in view from in front but slants to the left.

Placing the cable-needle stitches in back creates a right cross. Having the cable-needle stitches in the front results in a left cross. Mrs. Campbell in Seattle, Washington, taught me this wonderful mnemonic device many years ago: "I'll be right back." That is, having the cable-needle stitches in the back creates a right-cross cable.

Front or Back?
Some patterns do not refer to left or right slanting cables. Instead, the directions may say "front cross" or "back cross." If you get confused about what a cable looks like when stitches are held in front or in back, or if you want to see what the crossing will look like, use your hands and follow along.

If I put the first set of stitches on a cable needle and place them in front, knit the next set of stitches off the regular needle, then knit the stitches off the cable needle, what does the cable look like? Look at it this way: Put the first set of stitches on a cable needle and place them in front (place right hand forward; **Fig. 2a**); knit the next set of stitches off

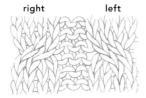

Fig. 1: Two types of cables, right and left.

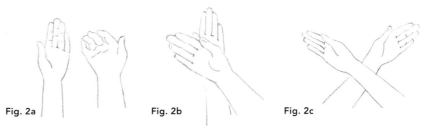

Fig. 2a–2c: Use your hands to see a left cross.

Fig. 3a   Fig. 3b   Fig. 3c

Fig. 3a–3c: Use your hands to see a right cross.

the regular needle (move left hand over to the right; **Fig. 2b**); knit the stitches off the cable needle (move right hand over and to the left; **Fig. 2c**). Look at your hands—they form a left slant.

Conversely, if I put the first set of stitches on a cable needle and place them in back, knit the next set of stitches off the regular needle, then knit the stitches off the cable needle, what does the cable look like? Put the first set of stitches on a cable needle and place them in back (place right hand to the back; **Fig. 3a**); knit the next set of stitches off the regular needle (move left hand right; **Fig. 3b**), then knit the stitches off the cable needle (place right hand under and to the left; **Fig. 3c**). According to your hands, it forms a right slant.

Front, back, left, right—it may sound confusing, but with this visualization trick, you can easily see which way your cables will cross.

Simple Cable Math

Cables come in pairs. This means that in order to change positions, they need someone to change positions with. The sets of stitches are a couple, and it takes

two to tango. For our purposes, let's call the components crossing over each other a set **(Fig. 4)**. In other words, a set of 2 stitches can cross over or under another set of 2 stitches, or a set of 4 stitches can cross over or under another set of 4 stitches. Thus, you need at least two sets of stitches to make a cross or cable. Note that two is an even number; most cables are comprised of an even number of stitches, though there will be exceptions.

One set of stitches usually contains the same number of stitches as the other set to be crossed with it. They tend to be equal partners. (This is not so all the time, as rules are made to be broken.)

They also tend to cross on even rows. We like to cross cables on the right-side rows when we are working back and forth. In order for the stitches to cross only on right-side rows, every "eventh" row after the initial crossing is another right-side row, worked with the cable facing you **(Fig. 5)**. Notice that there are an odd number of "plain" or non-crossing rows in between.

If the number of stitches in the cable (including stitches from all sets) is X, the cable tends to cross on every Xth row.

That is, a 4-stitch cable (2 over 2) generally crosses every fourth row, a 6-stitch cable (3 over 3) crosses every sixth row, an 8-stitch cable (4 over 4) gets crossed every eighth row, and so on.

There are exceptions to these rules of thumb, but they are true more often than not. Keep them in mind whether you're designing cables or keeping track of rows within a pattern.

Fig. 4: Sets of cable stitches.

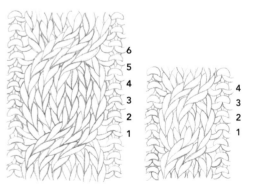

Fig. 5: Cables tend to cross on an "eventh" row.

CHARTING

A lot of people have conniptions about charts, but they are quite useful in presenting a picture of what stitches must be executed. You can see where you've been and where you have to go. Each box across equals one stitch, and each box up equals one row.

Traditional Charting

I suspect the problem most people have with charts is that although you turn your work when working back and forth, the chart only represents the front side of the work. To make it more challenging, the right-side rows are read from right to left, but the wrong-side rows are read from left to right. To further compound confusion, the stitches reverse themselves; a knit stitch on the right side becomes a purl stitch on the wrong side and vice versa. Consider the chart and directions at right **(Fig. 6)**.

If you squint or take off your glasses, you might discern from the chart that this is a left-crossing cable. It looks very little like what your knitting will ultimately be, and you cannot see the actual cable. So I came up with a shorthand method that is a lot more WYSIWYG (what you see is what you get). Using the notion of sets instead of the actual number of stitches, you can chart the movement or makeup of cables.

Cable Needles

To maneuver the stitches into their new order, we generally use a cable needle to move some stitches out of the way.

There are several types of cable needles on the market. They may be made of wood, metal, or plastic. Many favor wood or plastic for their light weight. Some are straight, some are bent, and others are curved. My personal favorite is the "hook" shape in any material. I slip the stitches on from the short end of the U and let them dangle. The U portion not only keeps the stitches from sliding off, it also helps "scrunch up" the stitches so that they are not spread out. This ensures a tighter, more gap-free cable. I then knit the stitches off the longer end of the U so that there's no need to place them back onto the left-hand needle, thus avoiding an extra step. Try out a few and see which you prefer.

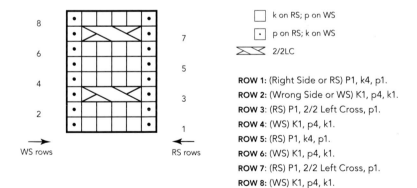

	k on RS; p on WS
.	p on RS; k on WS
⋈	2/2LC

ROW 1: (Right Side or RS) P1, k4, p1.
ROW 2: (Wrong Side or WS) K1, p4, k1.
ROW 3: (RS) P1, 2/2 Left Cross, p1.
ROW 4: (WS) K1, p4, k1.
ROW 5: (RS) P1, k4, p1.
ROW 6: (WS) K1, p4, k1.
ROW 7: (RS) P1, 2/2 Left Cross, p1.
ROW 8: (WS) K1, p4, k1.

WS rows   RS rows

Fig 6: The traditional method of charting a four-stitch rope cable.

Cables Without a Cable Needle

I cannot begin to count the number of cable needles I've lost in my lifetime, even on airplanes—it amazes me that I manage to lose a cable needle at 35,000 feet in an enclosed space. If you want to speed up your knitting and free yourself from needing a needle at all, practice cabling without a needle.

PINCH METHOD

Some people use the "pinch" method. To try this, take the stitches that would normally go on a cable needle and pinch them together with your fingers when you take them off the needles. **(Fig. A)**. (Take a deep breath; I know it's scary.) Now hold those stitches to the front or back according to the pattern as you work the stitches from the regular needle **(Fig. B)**. Replace the pinched stitches on the left needle, then knit them off **(Fig. C)**. Some people can knit these stitches directly off their fingers without having to replace them on the left needle, but it can be tricky. The fewer stitches to be pinched off, the easier this maneuver is, so start small. Begin with only 1 stitch for a 2-stitch (1/1) cable. Build up to 2 stitches for a 4-stitch cable. Once you feel more comfortable, work your way up to moving 3 and 4 stitches. (I haven't personally gotten up to 4 stitches yet, so for anything larger, I still use the old cable needle.)

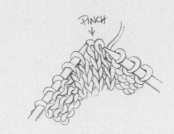

Fig. A

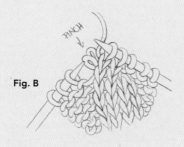

Fig. B

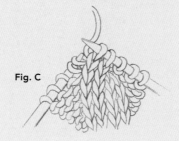

Fig. C

NEEDLE-TRANSFER METHOD

Another method is what I call the needle-transfer. Let's start small, with a simple 1/1 two-stitch cable. For a right cross, insert the right needle into the next 2 stitches on the left needle as if to knit them together and slip them from the left to right needle **(Fig. D)**. With the left needle behind the right, place the first of these 2 slipped stitches back onto the left needle **(Fig. E)**, then slip the second stitch back to the left needle **(Fig. F)**. (Remember to correct the stitch mount, as slipping the stitches knitwise twists them.) These stitches are now "pre-crossed"—they've already exchanged positions, so all you have to do is knit them one by one off the left needle in their new order.

For a left cross, slip the next 2 stitches from the left to the right needle as if to purl **(Fig. G)**. With the left needle in front of the right, insert the tip of the left needle into the first of these 2 slipped stitches and move it back onto the left needle **(Fig. H)**. Take the right needle out of these 2 stitches. Note that the second of these 2 stitches is not on any needle at this point; quickly move the floating stitch back onto left needle **(Fig. I)**. As for the right cross, these stitches are ready to be worked one by one in their new order.

For a larger cable, such as 4 stitches, set up for a right cross by slipping the four stitches to the right needle as if to knit them together. Insert the left needle from behind into the first 2, then slip the last 2 back onto the left needle. For the left cross, slip the 4 stitches onto the right needle as if to purl. Insert the left needle from the front into the first 2. Take the right needle out of the 4 stitches, then quickly place the last 2 back onto the left needle. Practice until you can maneuver 6 and even 8 stitches.

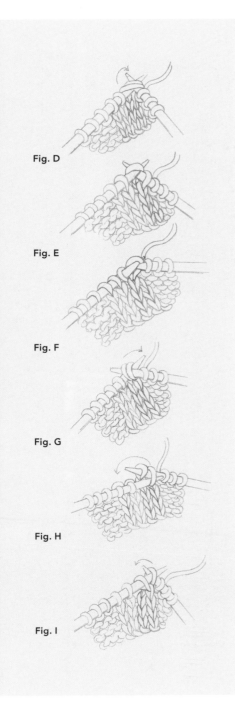

Fig. D

Fig. E

Fig. F

Fig. G

Fig. H

Fig. I

My Charting System

In my charting method, each box is equal to one set of stitches. You will need graph paper, a pencil, and a straightedge ruler; graph paper with four boxes to the inch is a wonderful size that is easy to see and easier to draw on. Begin by placing two dots in each box for two boxes across and about six boxes high (**Fig. 7**).

Now, just as in kindergarten, we will play "connect the dots." Begin with the bottom dots and draw four parallel lines straight up to the next boxes above (**Fig. 8**). *Draw two parallel lines diagonally from the lower right to the upper left (**Fig. 9**). Draw two more parallel lines diagonally from the lower left to the upper right, but do not draw over the

first set of diagonal lines (**Fig. 10**). Draw four more straight-up parallel lines up to the next boxes (**Fig. 11**). Repeat from * (**Fig. 12**). What you see is what you get. What does this look like? Hint—it's not DNA. I can even shade in each set or strand for further clarity (**Fig. 13**).

To further illustrate how my charting system relates to traditional charts, let's match up the equivalents (**Fig. 14**). Note that in my charting method the center of the "X" (or the crossing row of the cable) lands smack on the line of the graph paper. This line corresponds to the crossing row in the traditional chart. The vertical parallel lines are equal to the plain rows of the traditional chart.

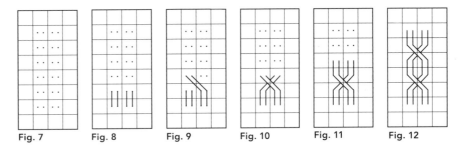

Fig. 7   Fig. 8   Fig. 9   Fig. 10   Fig. 11   Fig. 12

Fig. 7: Begin by drawing pairs of dots. **Figs. 8–12:** Connect the dots to form a new chart.

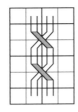

Fig 13: Finished versions of my charts can be shaded to show which stitches are on top.

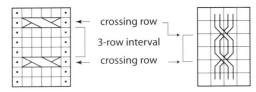

← crossing row
3-row interval
← crossing row

Fig. 14: Traditional and new charts of a rope cable.

Knitting from My Charts

My chart shows the directions of the cables; to translate them to knitting directions, fill in the number of stitches in the cables (and between the cables, if applicable. The formula for the former is (number of sets) x (stitches in each set) = number of stitches in the cable. By the way, look at how many boxes are saved because I don't have to chart out every single stitch and each and every row. I can even reuse this chart for a smaller version with fewer stitches or a larger version with more stitches!

This chart can then represent a cable of any number of stitches. It can represent a 6-stitch cable if each set or box equals 3 stitches, or it can represent a 10-stitch cable if each set or box equals 5 stitches **(Fig. 15)**. You can write numbers along the vertical lines to indicate the number of plain rows between crossing rows. To indicate the purl stitches that typically frame a cable worked in stockinette stitch, I leave an empty column between cables and write in "p1" or "p2" **(Fig. 16)**. To knit from the chart, just add in the number of stitches in the set and rows between crossings.

Notice that you use only one chart for both the big and little versions of the same cable pattern. It doesn't matter if this is a big, fat 12-stitch cable (6 over 6, with eleven rows between crossings, or crossing every twelfth row) or a tiny 2-stitch baby cable (1 over 1, with one row between crossings, or crossing every other row). The pattern is the same.

When a cable crosses the same way over and over again (such as this one, which crosses to the left), it is known typically as a rope cable. I don't care if it's a

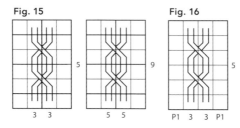

Fig. 15: Write the number of stitches per set at the bottom and the number of plain rows at the side.
Fig. 16: Write the number of purl stitches beside the cables.

big rope or a little rope; the pattern is still a rope. As Gertrude Stein wroted, a Rope is a Rope is a Rope [sic].

Using my charting method, I promise that if you can draw it, you can knit it—and you can really see what the cable will look like. You will also be your own cable designer. You, too, can come up with your own original, never-before-seen cable patterns. You will also come to understand the structure of cables better. You will even be able to look at an existing piece of knitting and figure out how it was done and how to reproduce it. Have you seen someone wearing a handsome cabled sweater and just wanted pull it apart to see how it was done? Now you can figure it out just by looking (without being so rude)! You can see cables in stitch dictionaries and decipher them more easily just by looking at the picture.

COMPLEX PATTERNS

All types, even of more complex cables, are really just based on the combinations of right cross and left cross. The cable on the bottom of page 15 is a left-cross rope cable with staggered

Fig. 17: Wave cable.
Fig. 18: Wave cable with its mirror image, forming lozenges.

crossing rows on every other cable, otherwise known as a half-drop. The half-drop is one of the most common variations on a simple cable.

The wave cable is only a right cross alternating with a left cross **(Fig. 17)**. Add the mirror image, a left cross first alternating with a right cross, to create lozenges **(Fig. 18)**.

This is the basis for the very common honeycomb pattern formed by placing a series of the same lozenges side by side **(Fig. 19)**. This is a standard in tons of Aran sweaters, including the Honeycomb V-neck Pullover (see page 24). (The names of patterns may vary by stitch dictionary, geographical region, and from one designer to another designer.) See how the line-by-line directions correspond with the chart?

STITCH FILE

Honeycomb Cable

CO 32 sts (8 sets × 4 sts in each set).

Work 8 rows in St st.

*FIRST CROSSING ROW: [Work 4/4 Left Cross (cn in front), work 4/4 Right Cross (cn in back)] 2 times.

Work 7 rows in St st.

SECOND CROSSING ROW: [Work 4/4 Right Cross (cn in back), work 4/4 Left Cross (cn in front)] 2 times.

Work 7 rows in St st.

Repeat from * for pattern.

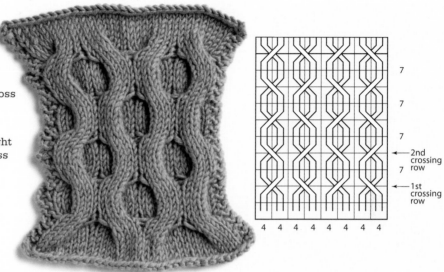

STITCH FILE

Half-Drop Left Rope Cable

CO 8 sets of sts.

Work in St st to first crossing row.

FIRST CROSSING ROW: [Work Left Cross, knit 2 sets even without crossing] 2 times.

Work in St st to next crossing row.

*SECOND CROSSING ROW: [Knit 2 sets without crossing, work Left Cross] 2 times.

Rep from * for pattern.

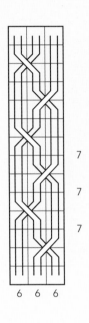

Braid Cable

CO 18 sts (3 strands × 6 sts in each strand).

Work 8 rows in St st.

*FIRST CROSSING ROW: Work 6/6 Right Cross (cn in back), k6 (work next 6 sts without crossing).

Work 7 rows in St st.

SECOND CROSSING ROW: K6 (work next 6 sts without crossing), work 6/6 Left Cross (cn in front).

Work 7 rows in stockinette stitch.

Repeat from * for pattern.

Braid Cables

I said before that in cables, it takes two to tango. But there can actually be more than two parties in a cable relationship.

As for braiding hair, you need three strands or sets for a braid cable. Looking at the Stitch File at left, you will see that the middle-position set will cross one way with the one on the right but will cross the other way with the one on the left. Just as for the honeycomb pattern, you can make this a smaller or larger braid by changing the numbers in each strand; adjust the number of rows between crossings accordingly.

To manipulate a braid for even more complex-looking patterns, just add more braids, the mirror image of the braid, or a half-drop. Adding more braids is self-explanatory; at the top of page 17 are four braids in a row for a total of twelve sets. In this case, the half-drop and the mirror image are the same, shown on the bottom of page 17. They consist of four braids: the braid and its mirror image, twice.

Many-stranded Cables

Why stop with a braid? Here are cables that use four or more sets of stitches. Notice that even though the sets change positions after crossing, they are still referred to by the fixed column position. Needless to say, you can add as many stitches in each set as you desire for a small or large pattern. Try your own variations with a half-drop or mirror image, or create a sampler piece on an afghan that incorporates all variations with purl columns stitches separating the variations.

STITCH FILE

Twelve-set Braid Cable

CO 12 sets of stitches (3 sets × number of sts in each set × 4 cables).

Work in St st to first crossing row.

*FIRST CROSSING ROW: [Work Right Cross (cn in back), knit next set without crossing] 4 times.

Work in St st to second crossing row.

SECOND CROSSING ROW: [Knit first set without crossing), work Left Cross (cn in front)] 4 times.

Work in St st to next crossing row.

Rep from * for pattern.

STITCH FILE

Twelve-set Mirrored or Half-drop Cable

CO 12 sets of stitches (3 sets × number of sts in each set × 4 cables).

Work in St st to first crossing row.

*FIRST CROSSING ROW: [Work Right Cross, work two sets without crossing, work Left Cross] 2 times.

Work in St st to next crossing row.

SECOND CROSSING ROW: [Work a set without crossing, work Left Cross, work Right Cross, work a set without crossing] 2 times.

Work in St st to next crossing row.

Rep from * for pattern.

Celtic Braid

CO 4 sets of sts.

Work in St st to first crossing row.

***FIRST CROSSING ROW:** Work Right Cross (cn in back) 2 times.

Work in St st to next crossing row.

SECOND CROSSING ROW: Knit 1 set without crossing, work Left Cross (cn in front), knit 1 set without crossing.

Work in St st to next crossing row.

Rep from * for pattern.

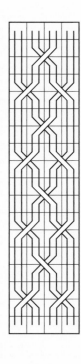

For the first four-strand cable above, the bottom crossing shows two pairs, with 1/2 and 3/4 both crossing right. On the next crossing row, 2/3 cross left, while 1 and 4 do not cross. The following crossing row has 1/2 and 3/4 both crossing to the right again. Repeating this pattern creates a four-strand or Celtic braid. The original pairs (1/2 and 3/4) always cross to the right, but the interim pair always crosses left.

Another variation (top of page 19) is for 1/2 and 3/4 to begin by crossing in opposite directions first (right, then left), then the center pair crosses left first. For the third and fourth crossings, all the pairs cross in the opposite direction. This variation creates rings that form with an X in the middle.

In the third variation (bottom of page 19), all of the cables begin by crossing in only one direction, to the right. (If all of the sets cross in only one direction—let's say right—they may be known as a spiral cable.) But imagine that at some point the cables begin to cross to the left. Alternate right crosses only, then left crosses only, up the cable. Then add the mirror image (see page 20). The cable pattern forms a diamond within another diamond, so I named this pattern Shadow Diamonds.

STITCH FILE

Crossed Rings Cable

CO 4 sets of sts.

Work in St st to first crossing row.

*FIRST CROSSING ROW: Work Right Cross (cn in back), work Left Cross (cn in front).

Work in St st to next crossing row.

SECOND CROSSING ROW: Knit 1 set without crossing, work Left Cross, knit 1 set without crossing.

Work in St st to next crossing row.

THIRD CROSSING ROW: Work Left Cross, work Right Cross.

Work in St st to next crossing row.

FOURTH CROSSING ROW: Knit 1 set without crossing, work Right Cross, knit 1 set without crossing.

Rep from * for pattern.

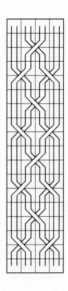

STITCH FILE

Half-Diamond Cable

CO 4 sets of sts.

Work in St st to first crossing row.

*FIRST CROSSING ROW: Work Right Cross (cn in back) 2 times.

Work in St st to second crossing row.

SECOND CROSSING ROW: Knit first set without crossing, work Right Cross, knit 1 set without crossing.

Work in St st to next crossing row.

Rep from * for pattern.

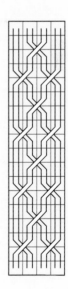

Shadow Diamond Cable

CO 8 sets of sts.

Work in St st to first crossing row.

*FIRST CROSSING ROW: Work Right Cross (cn in back) 2 times, work Left Cross (cn in front) 2 times.

Work in St st to second crossing row.

SECOND CROSSING ROW: Knit first set without crossing, work Right Cross, knit 2 sets without crossing, work Left Cross, knit 1 set without crossing.

Work in St st to next crossing row.

Rep from * 1 time.

**FIFTH CROSSING ROW: Work Left Cross 2 times, work Right Cross 2 times.

Work in St st to next crossing row.

SIXTH CROSSING ROW: Knit 1 set without crossing, work Left Cross 1 time, knit 2 sets without crossing, work Right Cross 1 time, knit 1 set without crossing.

Rep from ** 1 time.

STITCH FILE

A Cable Inspired by Gilligan's Island

CO 7 sets of sts.

Work in St st to first crossing row.

*FIRST CROSSING ROW: Work Right cross (cn in back) 3 times, knit 1 set without crossing.

Work in St st to next crossing row.

SECOND CROSSING ROW: Knit 1 set without crossing, work Left Cross 3 times.

Work in St st to next crossing row.

Rep from * for pattern.

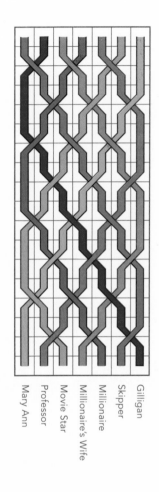

Mary Ann
Professor
Movie Star
Millionaire's Wife
Millionaire
Skipper
Gilligan

Push the envelope some more and explore cables with even more sets! In this sample, imagine Gilligan's Island. The first crossing row has Gilligan and the Skipper crossing right (positions 1 and 2), the millionaire and his wife crossing right (positions 3 and 4), the movie star and the professor crossing right (positions 5 and

6), and poor Mary Ann is left alone with no one to cross with (position 7). Don't feel so sorry for Mary Ann, though—Gilligan then declares that everyone changes partners and changes crossing direction.

Gilligan himself is left alone with no one to cross with on this next crossing row.

The Skipper crosses left with the millionaire (positions 2 and 3), the millionaire's wife crosses left with the movie star (positions 4 and 5), and the professor and Mary Ann cross left (positions 6 and 7). Repeat these two crossing rows, and you get the classic Basketweave (or Plaited or Lattice) cable pattern.

Double Crossings

The mirror image, the half-drop, and the repeat are three ways we've explored to adapt cable patterns for new designs. Another variation is the double-cross: take any given cable cross and repeat it. For example, start with a braid cable, but cross the middle set to the right twice before crossing the middle set to the left twice (**Fig. 19**). Below right are a few more. Can you figure what the original patterns were (**Fig. 20–22**)?

VARYING CROSSING ROWS

Although cables tend to cross after the same number of rows as there are stitches in the cable, this is not a hard and fast rule. Let me tell you the tale of the traveling cable (**Fig. 23**).

There is a couple very much in love. They cross on Row 1, and very shortly thereafter they cross again, on Row 5.

She has to go on the road for business, though, so there is a long stretch where they do not cross at all. When she returns, they fall into each other's arms and cross on Row 13 and soon after on Row 17. She takes another road trip and there's another hiatus, but she comes home and they cross on Rows 25 and 29. Then he goes away and there's a while before they can cross again. You get the idea—here is a creative use of different crossing rows. This will be used later in the Reversible-cuff Cabled Socks on page 54 with a half-drop formation (**Fig. 24**), but there are other variations, including a repeat pattern (**Fig. 25**) and a mirror-image version (**Fig. 26**).

The previous example showed cables crossing at the same set of intervals (every fourth and eighth rows), but there are other variations, such as rows between cable crossings. Here's another love story of cables crossing at lessening and then increasing intervals (**Fig. 27**): Boy meets girl; they fall in love and cross on Row 1. They date regularly and cross on Row 5. They get engaged and cross on Row 11. They get married and cross on Row 19. They have children and cross on Row 29. They seek counseling and cross on Row 37. They get divorced and cross on Row 43. They're single again and cross on Row 47. The romantic life of cables is another creative way to envision varying crossing rows.

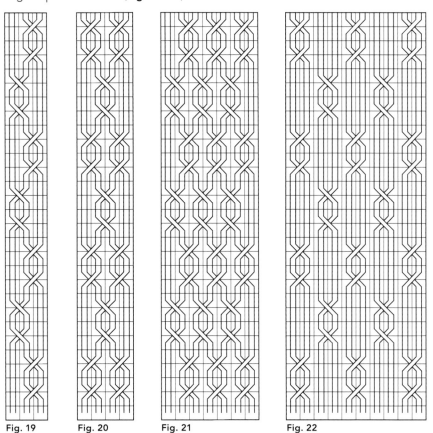

Fig. 19   Fig. 20   Fig. 21   Fig. 22

Fig. 19: Double-cross braid. **Fig. 20:** Double-cross Celtic braid. **Fig. 21:** Double-cross basketweave.
Fig. 22: Double-cross half-drop right ropes.

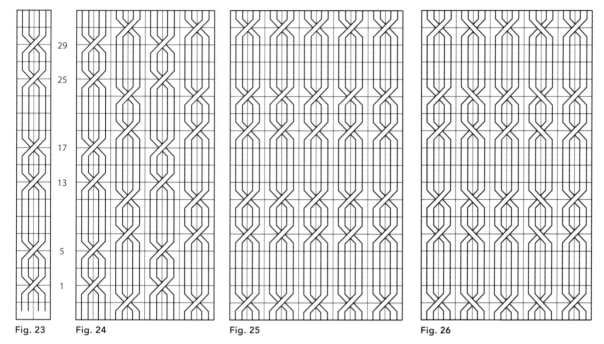

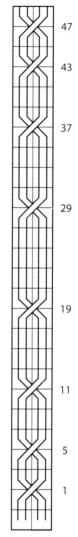

Fig. 23: Traveling Couple Cable. **Fig. 24:** Traveling Couple with half-drop. **Fig 25:** Traveling Couple repeated. **Fig. 26:** Traveling Couple with mirror image.

As you can see, a lot of complicated-looking cable patterns are nothing but manipulations of a single unit. I love this: the pattern just looks hard but is really quite simple. Fool your knitting friends—wipe your brow and pretend it's a lot of work. If you can find and understand the basic unit, you can then analyze and easily decipher how the whole cable works.

Use my new system as a guide or as a general planner to see the "big picture," but you may want to revert back to the old system to see the finer details. (The charts used for the projects in this book use the traditional style, but it may help you to practice drawing them for yourself in my new charting system.)

Fig. 27: Waxing and waning cables.

FINISHED MEASUREMENTS

35 (38, 40½, 43½)" (89 [96.5, 103, 110.5] cm) bust circumference and 21¼ (21¼, 23, 23)" (54 [54, 58.5, 58.5] cm) long, to be worn with standard ease. Sweater shown measures 38" (96.5 cm).

YARN

Worsted (Medium #4).
Shown here: Mission Falls 1824 Wool (100% superwash merino; 85 yd [78 m]/50 g): Pistachio #028, 14 (15, 16, 17) skeins.

NEEDLES

U.S. size 5 (3.75 mm): straight and 16" (40 cm) circular (cir). U.S. size 7 (4.5 mm): Straight. Adjust needle sizes if necessary to obtain the correct gauge.

NOTIONS

Removable stitch markers (m); cable needle (cn); tapestry needle.

GAUGE

8-st rep of Honeycomb cabled center panel = 1½" (3.2 cm).
10-st Rope Cable patt = 1¾" (4.5 cm).
12 sts (3 reps) of Mini-Honeycomb side panel = 2¼" (5.5 cm).
26 rows = 4" (10 cm) in all patterns, measured after steam blocking.

HONEYCOMB
v-neck pullover

This sweater features classic motifs from traditional Aran sweaters in a modern design. It's a classic look, so make more than one and wear them for decades to come. The shape is flattering on both guys and gals. Make this alone or as a companion piece to the Honeycomb Scarf on page 50. Note the engineering behind the organic-looking neckline decreases.

NOTES

Stitch markers indicate the edges of stitch patterns; slip markers (sl m) as you come to them.
V-neck decreases are specifically engineered to the stitch pattern, making the row count specific as well. Be aware to total lengths and adjust accordingly.

stitch guide

LC (1 over 1 Left Cross): Sl 1 st to cn and hold in front, k1, k1 from cn.

RC (1 over 1 Right Cross): Sl 1 st to cn and hold in back, k1, k1 from cn.

2/2LC (2 over 2 Left Cross): Sl 2 sts to cn and hold in front, k2, k2 from cn.

2/2RC (2 over 2 Right Cross): Sl 2 sts to cn and hold in back, k2, k2 from cn.

4/4LC (4 over 4 Left Cross): Sl 4 sts to cn and hold in front, k4, k4 from cn.

4/4RC (4 over 4 Right Cross): Sl 4 sts to cn and hold in back, k4, k4 from cn.

2/2 LC dec (2 over 2 Left Cross decrease): Sl 2 sts to cn and hold in front, [knit 1 st from cn tog with 1 st from left needle] twice—2 sts dec'd.

2/2RC dec (2 over 2 Right Cross decrease): Sl 2 sts to cn and hold in back, [knit 1 st from cn tog with 1 st from left needle] twice—2 sts dec'd.

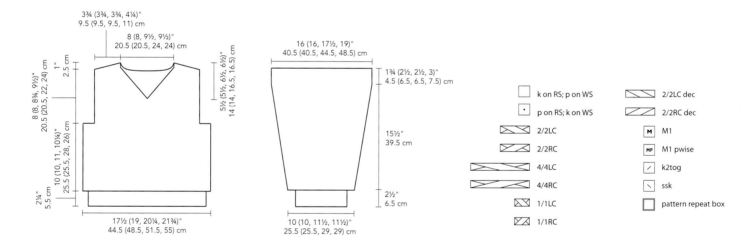

☐	k on RS; p on WS	⧄	2/2LC dec
·	p on RS; k on WS	⧄	2/2RC dec
⬚	2/2LC	M	M1
⬚	2/2RC	MP	M1 pwise
⬚	4/4LC	╱	k2tog
⬚	4/4RC	╲	ssk
⬚	1/1LC	☐	pattern repeat box
⬚	1/1RC		

Body Setup Row

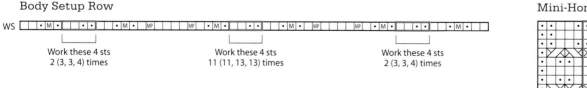

WS

Work these 4 sts
2 (3, 3, 4) times

Work these 4 sts
11 (11, 13, 13) times

Work these 4 sts
2 (3, 3, 4) times

Mini-Honeycomb

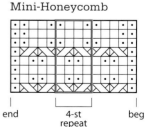

end   4-st
repeat   beg

BACK

With smaller straight needles, CO 94 (102, 110, 118) sts.

Ribbing

Row 1 and all odd-numbered rows: (WS) P2, [k2, p2] to end.
Row 2 and all even-numbered rows: K2, [p2, k2] to end.
Rep Rows 1 and 2 until ribbing measures 2¼" (5.5 cm), ending after a RS row.

Body

Next row: (WS; inc row) With larger needles, work Body Setup Row following chart—104 (112, 120, 128) sts.
Next row: K2, p1, place marker (pm), work Mini-Honeycomb over next 14 (18, 18, 22) sts, pm, work Right Rope over next 10 sts, pm, work Honeycomb over next 50 (50, 58, 58) sts, pm, work Left Rope over next 10 sts, pm, work Mini-Honeycomb over next 14 (18, 18, 22) sts, pm, p1, k2.
Work in patt as established until piece measures 12¼ (12¼, 13¼, 12½)" (31 [31, 33.5, 32] cm), ending after a WS row.

Shape Armholes

Next row: (RS) BO 8 (12, 12, 14) sts, k1, p1, work in patt to end—96 (100, 108, 114) sts rem.
Next row: (WS) BO 8 (12, 12, 14) sts, p1, k1, work in patt to end—88 (88, 96, 100) sts rem.
Next row: K2, p1, work in patt to last 3 sts, p1, k2.
Next row: P2, k1, work in patt to last 3 sts, p1, k2.
Continue in patt as established until armholes measure 7¾ (7¾, 8½, 9¼)" (19.5 [19.5, 21.5, 23.5] cm), ending after a RS row.

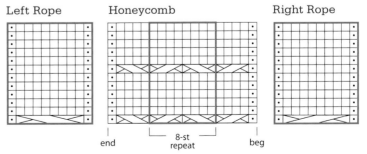

Left Rope   Honeycomb   Right Rope

end   8-st repeat   beg

Chart Legend

□	k on RS; p on WS
·	p on RS; k on WS
⟋⟍	2/2LC
⟍⟋	2/2RC
⟋⟍	4/4LC
⟍⟋	4/4RC
⟋⟍	1/1LC
⟍⟋	1/1RC
⟍⟋	2/2LC dec
⟍⟋	2/2RC dec
M	M1
MP	M1 pwise
⟋	k2tog
⟍	ssk
□	pattern repeat box

Neck Decrease

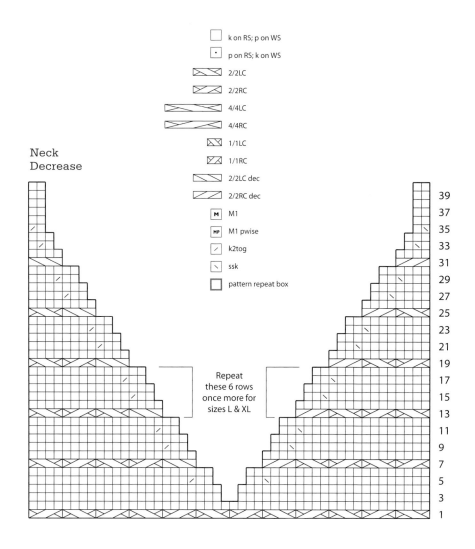

Repeat these 6 rows once more for sizes L & XL

Sleeve Setup Row

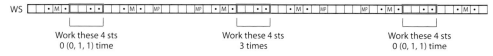

Work these 4 sts 0 (0, 1, 1) time

Work these 4 sts 3 times

Work these 4 sts 0 (0, 1, 1) time

Shape Back Neck

Next row: (WS) Work 28 (28, 28, 30) sts in patt, join a new ball of yarn and BO 32 (32, 40, 40) sts, work to end. *Note:* Read directions completely before proceeding, as several actions are performed at the same time.

Work shoulders separately as foll: BO 3 sts from each neck edge over the next 2 rows, BO 2 sts from each neck edge over the next 2 rows, then dec 1 st at each neck edge on next RS row.

Shape Shoulders

At the same time, when armholes measure 8 (8, 8¾, 9½)" (20.5 [20.5, 22, 24] cm), BO 6 sts from each shoulder edge one (one, one, three) time(s), then BO 5 sts from each shoulder edge two (two, two, zero) time(s). BO rem 6 sts.

FRONT

Work as for Back until armholes measure about 3½ (3½, 3¼, 4)" (9 [9, 8.5, 10] cm), ending after Honeycomb Row 8. Piece measures about 15¾ (15¾, 16½, 16½)" (40 [40, 42, 42] cm).

Shape Front Neck

Work first 43 (43, 47, 49) sts in patt as established, join a new ball of yarn and BO 2 sts, work in patt to end.

Continuing in patt as established and working shoulders separately, work Neck Decrease chart.

Shape Shoulders

At the same time, when armholes measure 8 (8, 8¾, 9½)" (20.5 [20.5, 22, 24] cm), shape shoulders as for Back.

SLEEVES

With smaller straight needles, CO 46 (46, 54, 54) sts.

Ribbing
Work Ribbing as for back for 2½" (6.5 cm), ending after a RS row.

Arm
Next row: (WS; inc row) With larger needles, work Sleeve Setup Row following chart—56 (56, 64, 64) sts.

Next row: K2, p1, pm, work Mini-Honeycomb over 6 (6, 10, 10) sts, pm, work Right Rope over 10 sts, pm, work Honeycomb over 18 sts, pm, work Left Rope over 10 sts, pm, work Mini-Honeycomb over 6 (6, 10, 10) sts, pm, p1, k2. Work in patt as established and *at the same time* M1 after first 2 and before last 2 St sts at each end every 4th row 3 (3, 3, 14) times, then every 6th row 13 (13, 13, 6) times, incorporating inc'd sts into Mini-Honeycomb patt—88 (88, 96, 104) sts.

Work even until piece measures 18" (45.5 cm). Mark each end of last row with removable markers to indicate top of underarm below sleeve cap.

Work even for 1¾ (2½, 2½, 3)" (4.5 [6.5, 6.5, 7.5] cm), ending after a WS row; piece measures 19¾ (20½, 20½, 21)" (50 [52, 52, 53.5] cm). BO in patt.

FINISHING

Steam block pieces to measurements. Sew shoulder seams. Sew top of sleeves to armholes. Sew straight portion at top of sleeves (above markers) to BO armhole sts. Sew side and sleeve seams.

Neck Trim
With RS facing, smaller cir needle, and beg at right shoulder seam, pick up and knit (see Glossary) 50 (50, 58, 58) sts evenly along Back Neck, 38 (38, 42, 42) sts along Left Neck edge, pm, pick up and knit 2 sts over center BO sts, 38 (38, 42, 42) sts along Right Neck edge, pm for beg of rnd—128 (128, 144, 144) sts. Pm between 2 center sts.

Join for working in the rnd. Work [k2, p2] ribbing as foll, making sure to work 1 st before and after m as k1 every rnd.

Next rnd: (dec rnd) Work in patt to 3 sts before center m, p1, k2tog, ssk, p1, work in patt to end—126 (126, 142, 142) sts rem.

Work 1 rnd in patt.

Next rnd: Work in patt to 2 sts before m, k2tog, ssk, work in patt to end—124 (124, 140, 140) sts rem.

Work 1 rnd in patt.

Next rnd: Work in patt to 3 sts before m, k1, k2tog, ssk, work in patt to end—122 (122, 138, 138) sts rem.

Work 1 rnd in patt.

Next rnd: Work in patt to 2 sts before m, k2tog, ssk, work in patt to end—120 (120, 136, 136) sts rem.

Work 1 rnd in patt.

BO in patt. Weave in loose ends.

wide-rib cables

It is often said that cables are nothing but ribbing. If a cable is worked primarily in stockinette stitch with reverse stockinette stitch on each side, is it not in essence ribbing? After all, if you alternate knits and purls, you get ribbing. Knowing that ribbing and cables are closely related gives us an opportunity to take cables to a new place—the "wrong" side.

THE BACK ISSUE

The cable below **(Fig. 1)** is basically a [k6, p3] rib with a cable in the k6 area. In any ribbing pattern, the vertical lines are known as wales, whether they be a stack of knits or a stack of purls. Think of corduroy, which is often described by wales. Each knit wale rib is a cable.

Even if the stitches between the cables are not reverse stockinette but instead seed or even garter stitch, the pattern is still a rib. As long as there are distinct wales, especially knit wales, the cable is a rib that happens to be undulating back and forth. Notice how the knits stand out and the purls recede. Even with garter or seed stitch on each side of it, a knit wale still protrudes. It's the nature of the stitch.

Wider cable patterns, such as a honeycomb or the pattern below, may not be easy to see as a rib but as an allover cable pattern. However, in the Honeycomb V-neck Pullover on page 24, the wide honeycomb is still flanked on both sides by reverse stockinette stitches followed by stockinette rope cables. Taken as a whole, this pattern can be considered a [p2, k8, p2, k48, p2, k8, p2] rib! Remember this above anything else: The back of knit is purl, and vice versa—the back of purl is knit. Ribs offer a chance at reversibility.

CREATING REVERSIBILITY

Reversibility is desirable in projects such as scarves and stoles and afghans. A reversible piece can be tossed around with the backside showing, as it is every bit as presentable as the front side. But the back of a typical cable is not very presentable and doesn't bear much resemblance to the front.

This puzzled me. A pair of crossed fingers is very much like a cable: instead of index, then middle finger, you've got middle finger, then index. Now turn your hand over and look at it from front and back. Are your fingers still crossed?

Fig. 1: [3/3 left cross, p3] ribbing.

Fig. 2: Back of cable.

Of course they are. It seemed to me that a cable should work the same way.

So why isn't a cable visible on both sides? If you look at the back of a cable, you see reverse stockinette. The cable, worked in smooth stockinette, is easy to see from the front, but the lumpy, bumpy purls on the back prevent you from seeing the cable **(Fig. 2)**. It's as though the back of your hand were covered with big zits and you couldn't see your fingers crossed as a result!

Yet looking at the back of this swatch, notice that the reverse stockinette from the front becomes stockinette on the back. Aha! There are hidden purl cables (or crossed purl wales) that recede and stand-out knit cables (or crossed knit wales) that are visible. You just don't see the hidden crossed purl cables because they are lumpy-bumpy (a technical term). But notice that, just as for all ribbing, the reverse stockinette on the front becomes stockinette on the back. This creates an opportunity to work a cable on this side! If you work a cable within each "rib" section, be it a knit wale or a purl wale, you will create cables on each side, making the piece reversible. This method of creating a cable in each wale of a wide rib is not new; I've seen fifty-year-old patterns that use this technique.

When you look at a knit cable popping out of the fabric, remember that the back is a purl cable, though the crossed stitches are hidden from view. When seeing a cable receding in purl stitches, it becomes visible as a knit cable on the other side. By alternating some knit

FRONT

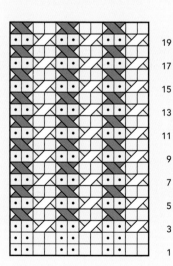

BACK

Baby Reversible Cable

CO 12 sts.

ROWS 1 AND 2: (set-up row) [K2, p2] to end.

ROW 3: [1/1 Right Cross, p2] to end.

ROW 4: [1/1 Left Cross, p2] to end.

Rep Rows 3 and 4 for patt.

☐ k on RS; p on WS

▪ p on RS; k on WS

⟋⟋ 1/1RC on RS; sl 1 st onto cn, hold in back, k1, k1 from cn

⟍⟍ 1/1LC on WS; sl 1 st onto cn, hold in front, k1, k1 from cn

Identical vs Fraternal Reversibility

For the sample at left, we could have worked the same cable on both sides, but they alternate left and right to illustrate that there are two kinds of reversibilities. Just as there are two kinds of twins, I refer to these as identical or fraternal reversibles. In the former, the back looks exactly like the front. In the latter, the back looks different than the front, but both sides are still presentable.

cables and some purl cables across a piece, there will always be some visible knit stitches to show cables on either side—hence reversibility.

To make a reversible cable pattern, the rib must be at least [k2, p2] (or 2x2), because you need at least 2 stitches in order to create a cable. In a 2x2 rib, you can make a small "baby" cable in each wale. Try it for yourself—work 2x2 rib and add a cable wherever you see 2 knit stitches in a row.

Why do we only cross on the knit stitches? In other words, why not work one row of 1/1 crosses over pairs of knits and purls, then work the next row as [k2, p2] across? Conceivably, we could cross the purl stitches when they face us, but we usually don't. For one thing, most of us like to see the cable clearly as we cross it, and the cable is most visible on the knit side. Another reason is that working all the cables on a single row creates quite a lot of "pull" on all the stitches. I like to stagger the crossings from one side to the other for this reason.

Notice that every one of the cables crossed in this sample crosses every other row. There are 2 stitches in this cable,

and a 2-stitch cable typically crosses every other row. So even though you are working crosses on every row, the purl stitches between crossings are the "plain" row for the cables of the other side.

Stitch Multiples

When designing with reversible cables, keep stitch multiples in mind. If you want to substitute a 1/1 reversible cable for a standard rib in a turtleneck, and the pattern calls for working the neck over 90 stitches, a 2x2 rib won't work without modifications. A [k2, p2] rib is a multiple of 4 stitches, and 90 is not a multiple of 4; to make it work, pick up 92 or even 96

stitches to maintain the pattern multiple. The stitch multiple for [k4, p4] rib is 8, and the stitch multiple for [k6, p6] rib is 12.

In a flat piece such as a stole or an afghan, the pattern tends to be symmetrical (**Fig. 3**). If a piece begins with k4, most of us will want the piece to end with k4. To make this symmetrical, add 4 stitches to your multiple of 8. For 6x6 rib, it will be a multiple of 12 plus an extra 6. (This does not include any edge trims or selvedge stitches.)

On the back, though, this change will make the piece begin and end with p4, making it a less than identical reverse.

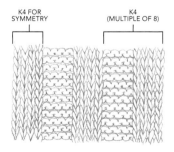 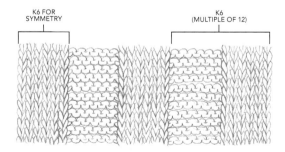

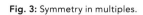

Fig. 3: Symmetry in multiples.

Cable Sizes

What if you wanted a larger cable than 1 over 1 from a 2x2 rib **(Fig. 4a)**? Other than using thicker yarns and larger needles, the easiest way is to make the ribs wider. Although the crossing sets of a cable tend to be equal partners with the same number of stitches in each set, you can actually work 3x3 ribs in which each wale is a single stitch crossed over the other 2 stitches or vice versa **(Fig. 4b)**. The next largest cable is made of 4 stitches, or 2 over 2, for which you would need a [k4, p4] rib **(Fig. 4c)**. The next possibility is a cable that crosses 3 over 3 in 6x6 rib **(Fig. 4d)**.

Notice that as the ribs get wider, the wrong sides of the cables begin to look different than plain reverse stockinette stitch, and you can actually see that it is a crossed purl cable. Some knitters are bothered by this, but others like the extra texture. If you don't like this effect, stick to smaller cables.

One thing you can't see is that the smaller cables stretch more easily, while the larger cables restrict stretch. With a larger distance to span, the crossing stitches hinder the give of the fabric. For a non-stretchy piece such as an afghan or a stole, wider cables are fine, but for items that require stretch such as sock tops or turtlenecks, keep to the smaller cables.

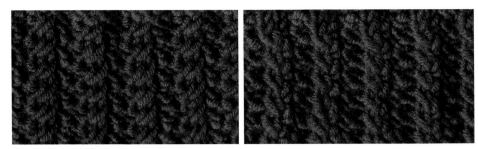

Fig. 4a: Front and back views of 1/1 cables in 2x2 rib.

Fig. 4b: Front and back views of 1/2 cables in 3x3 rib.

Fig. 4c: Front and back views of 2/2 cables in 4x4 rib.

Fig. 4d: Front and back views of 3/3 cables in 6x6 rib.

Fig 5: The Widening Rib Scarf is a fraternal reversible, with different stitch multiples and crossing rows on each side.

Keeping Track of Differing Crossing Rows

As the number of stitches in the cable increases, so do the intervals between crossing rows. But what happens when you mix and match? There's no need to restrain yourself to only 2-stitch, 4-stitch, or 6-stitch cables. The Widening-Rib Cabled Scarf on page 36 mixes cables of varying widths, creating a fraternal reversible where one side is not identical to the other side.

This kind of mixing requires you to keep track of different crossing rows for each cable. The 2-stitch cables (1 over 1) are crossed every other row, the 4-stitch cables (2 over 2) are crossed every fourth row, and the 6-stitch cables (3 over 3) are crossed every sixth row.

To effectively keep track of all the different crossing rows, I strongly recommend learning to recognize your knitting. Train yourself to see what row you are on rather than having to remember the pattern or sequence. This is often referred to as "reading your knitting," and it is an exceptionally useful skill to develop.

To help keep track, some knitters use different row counters. There are electronic ones on the market that can keep track of three different sets of rows. Some use the old-fashioned marks on paper, but alas, pieces of paper can get lost. Try a method that my friend Claire Gregorcyk suggests for counting rows: Set out as many M&M candies as there are rows before the next cable crossing, using plain for every 6th row and peanuts for every 4th row (or whatever number is needed). Eat one after every row. Once they're gone, work the cable and lay out another set. While not for the diet-conscious, this does indeed give you an incentive to work faster, and even the most absent-minded knitter probably won't forget to mark the end of the row. (Just make sure the kids aren't around to eat your markers.)

So take advantage of the reversibility of ribbing to add cables on both sides of your garment! It may not be exactly the same on both sides, but fraternal reversibility can make a scarf, blanket, or other piece attractively cabled any way you look at it.

Cables in the Round

When you work circularly, the wrong side never faces you, so you never see the back of the purls (which are knits on that side). If you're working reversibly, you have no choice but to cross the knits on one round, then cross the stitches as purls on another round for the knit cable that will be shown on the other side.

WIDENING-RIB
cabled scarf

Everyone needs one good cashmere scarf. Simple enough to make for several gifts (and for yourself) yet interesting to knit, this scarf will look great in a wide range of colors. It's also quick work in a chunky yarn and large needles. Make a larger version for a stole; with even more repeats you've got one luxurious afghan.

FINISHED SIZES
6¾ (16½, 45)" (17 [42, 114.5] cm) wide and 68" (172.5 cm) long. Scarf shown measures 6¾" (17 cm) wide.

YARN
Chunky (Bulky #5).
Shown here: Karabella Supercashmere (100% cashmere, 81 yd [75 m]/50 g): Olive #73, 5 (11, 30) skeins.

NEEDLES
U.S. sizes 9 (5.5 mm) and 10½ (6.5 mm). Adjust needle size if necessary to obtain the correct gauge.

NOTIONS
Cable needle (cn); tapestry needle.

GAUGE
1/1RC = ½" (1.3 cm).
2/2RC = ¾" (2 cm).
3/3RC = 1¼" (3 cm).
One 24-st rep = 4¾" (12 cm).

NOTES

Since this is a reversible piece and worked in an animal fiber, use the spit-splice (see Glossary) to join balls of yarn.
Markers indicate garter st side borders. Slip markers (sl m) as you come to them.
Although there is no true wrong side of the scarf, the sides are designated as RS and WS for clarification.

stitch guide

1/1RC (1 over 1 Right Cross): Sl 1 st to cn and hold in back of work, k1, k1 from cn.

2/2RC (2 over 2 Right Cross): Sl 2 sts to cn and hold in back of work, k2, k2 from cn.

3/3RC (3 over 3 Right Cross): Sl 3 sts to cn and hold in back of work, k3, k3 from cn.

Widening Ribs Pattern

(MULTIPLE OF 24 STS + 12)

ROW 1: (WS; Side A) Sl 1 purlwise (pwise) with yarn in front (wyf), k1, p1, *k2, p2, k2, p4, k2, p6, k2, p4; rep from * to last 9 sts, k2, p2, k2, p1, k1, p1.

ROW 2: (RS; Side B) Sl 1 knitwise (kwise) with yarn in back (wyb), p1, k1, *p2, k2, p2, k4, p2, k6, p2, k4; rep from * to last 9 sts, p2, k2, p2, k1, p1, k1.

ROWS 3 AND ALL WS (SIDE A) ROWS: Sl 1 pwise wyf, k1, p1, *1/1RC, p2, 1/1RC, p4, 1/1RC, p6, 1/1RC, p4; rep from * to last 9 sts, 1/1RC, p2, 1/1RC, p1, k1, p1.

ROW 4: Sl 1 knitwise (kwise) wyb, p1, k1, *p2, 1/1RC, p2, 2/2RC, p2, 3/3RC, p2, 2/2RC; rep from * to last 9 sts, p2, 1/1RC, p2, k1, p1, k1.

ROW 6: Sl 1 knitwise (kwise) wyb, p1, k1, * p2, 1/1RC, p2, k4, p2, k6, p2, k4; rep from * to last 9 sts, p2, 1/1RC, p2, k1, p1, k1.

ROW 8: Sl 1 knitwise (kwise) wyb, p1, k1, * p2, 1/1RC, p2, 2/2RC, p2, k6, p2, 2/2RC; rep from * to last 9 sts, p2, 1/1RC, p2, k1, p1, k1.

ROW 10: Sl 1 knitwise (kwise) wyb, p1, k1, * p2, 1/1RS, p2, k4, p2, 3/3RC, p2, k4; rep from * to last 9 sts, p2, 1/1RC, p2, k1, p1, k1.

ROW 12: Rep Row 8.

ROW 14: Rep Row 6.

Rep Rows 3–14 for patt.

SCARF

With smaller needles, CO 36 (84, 228) sts.
   Work Rows 1 and 2 of Widening Ribs patt (see Chart or Stitch Guide).
   Change to larger needles. Work Rows 3–14 of patt until piece measures 67½" (171.5 cm), ending after Row 4 of patt
   Change to smaller needles. Work Rows 1 and 2 of patt.
   BO tightly in patt.

Finishing
Block piece to measurements. Weave in ends.

Widening-ribs

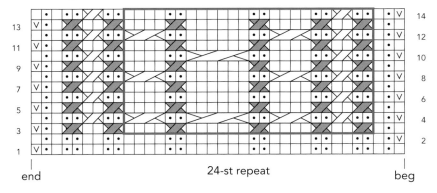

end · 24-st repeat · beg

☐ k on RS; p on WS

• p on RS; k on WS

∨ sl 1 wyb on RS; sl 1 wyf on WS

⧄⧄ 1/1RC on RS; sl 1 st onto cn, hold in back, k1, k1 from cn

⧄⧄ 1/1RC on WS; sl 1 st onto cn, hold in back, k1, k1 from cn

⧄ 2/2RC on RS; sl 2 sts onto cn, hold in back, k2, k2 from cn

⧄ 3/3RC on RS; sl 3 sts onto cn, hold in back, k3, k3 from cn

☐ pattern repeat box

ribbed
reversible cables

Now you see that you can make reversible cables in which the wale of the rib, be it a knit or a purl rib, is its own cable. But for real reversibility, I want the same cable cross to be visible on both sides. Knowing that the lumpy purl stitches that form the back of stockinette stitch get in the way of visibility, I experimented with reversible stitches. I first tried garter stitch but the cable was ugly on both sides, and with lumpy purl stitches on both sides, neither side showed the cable nicely. Back to the drawing board, this time with the knowledge that the reversible stitch needed to appear smooth on both sides. That's when it struck me to use ribbing as the basis for cables.

STITCH FILE

WHY RIBBING?

Ribbing appears smooth on both sides and is a reversible stitch. Ribs also have the advantage of vertical ridges that define the stitches. Columns of stockinette stitches stacked on top of each other alternate with reverse stockinette stitches also stacked one atop the other. On the back, the knit stitches of one side become purl stitches, and vice versa.

Ribbing looks deceptively like stockinette but with half the numbers—4 stitches of [k1, p1] rib look like only 2 stockinette stitches. The knits stand out as the purls recede. If we cable these reversible stitches, we should have a reversible cable.

On the ribbed cable sample at right, the same cable crossing is in full view from both front and back! The cable also crosses in the same direction, forming a left cross on both sides. Cross your fingers again to see the direction, then look at the other side of the hand—same cross! This is a true identical reversible. Although the cable is made of 8 stitches (4 over 4), it looks like 4 stitches (2 over 2). The receding purls do not show. The added bonus is that you only have to cross once in order for this cable to show up on both sides. In the previous method, you have to cross cables on each side, which doubles the number of cables you have to work.

Why don't the cables show on the other side? Because of the purls. How can we get rid of the purls? By cabling in ribbing. It's amazingly simple.

1×1 Ribbed Cable

CO 12 sts.

SET-UP ROW: K2 (selvedge), [k1, p1] 4 times, k2 (selvedge).

Rep last row until piece measures 1" (2.5 cm).

ROW 1: (cable row) K2, sl 4 sts to cn and hold in front, [k1, p1, k1, p1] from left needle, [k1, p1, k1, p1] from cn, k2.

ROWS 2–8: Rep set-up row.

Rep Rows 1–8 for patt.

Tidy Edges

Note that in the sample at right there are two additional selvedge or edge stitches on each side. Most pieces are either finished with an edging or seamed, so I like to add such selvedges for neater edges. These garter-stitch selvedges can serve as a self-trim so that no other trim is necessary. To really neaten the side edges, try slipping the first stitch of every row as if to purl with the yarn in front, then bringing the yarn to the back to knit the second stitch. This forms what is known as a slip-stitch chain selvedge, which is shown at the top of the swatch.

Stitch Multiples

Since the basis of ribbed reversible cables, or "ribbles" for short, is 1x1 or [k1, p1] rib, there are some stitch count considerations. The smallest cable possible is a 2-stitch cable, 1 stitch crossed over another. But working a 1/1 cable in ribbing would mean crossing a knit over or under a purl, which would not maintain the rib pattern.

By definition, it takes at least 2 stitches to create a rib, at least 1 knit and at least 1 purl, for a multiple of 2. In order for each crossing set to be in rib, each set must have at least 2 stitches. The smallest cable possible in 1x1 rib is a 4-stitch cable in which a set of 2 stitches (k1, p1) crosses over another set of 2 stitches (k1, p1). Each set in a 1x1 ribbed cable must be a multiple of 2. The next largest size ribbed cable is 4 over 4 for an 8-stitch cable, or [k1, p1, k1, p1] crossed over [k1, p1, k1, p1]. See the tables below for the number of stitches required for ribbles.

To maintain the ribbing pattern, the number of stitches in each set to cross must be even. If you tried to cross 3 ribbing stitches, such as [k1, p1, k1], they would be [p1, k1, p1] on the back—not symmetrical. The cross would also break up the ribbing pattern. You can cross 222 stitches over 222 stitches as long as each crossing set is a multiple of 2. (Actually, I'd like to see such a cable.)

OTHER RIBS

Knit 1, purl 1 rib is hardly the only rib available. Almost as common is [k2, p2] or 2x2 rib, which has a repeat or stitch multiple of 4. The smallest cable possible in 2x2 rib without breaking pattern is 4 over 4 for 8 stitches total, or [k2, p2] crossed over [k2, p2]. The next largest cable in 2x2 rib is 16 stitches, or [k2, p2, k2, p2] crossed over [k2, p2, k2, p2]. The smallest set for any cable worked in a 2x2 rib must be a multiple of 4.

Stitch Multiples for 1×1 Ribbed Cables

stitches of cable crossings	total number of stitches in cable
2 over 2	4
4 over 4	8
6 over 6	12
8 over 8	16
10 over 10	20
12 over 12	24

Stitch Multiples for 2×2 Ribbed Cables

stitches of cable crossings	total number of stitches in cable
4 over 4	8
8 over 8	16
12 over 12	24

2×2 Ribbed Cable

CO 12 sts.

SET-UP ROW: Sl 1 pwise wyf, k1 (selvedge), [k2, p2] twice, k2 (selvedge).

Rep last row until piece measures about 1" (2.5 cm).

ROW 1: (cable row) Sl 1 pwise wyf, k1, sl 4 sts to cn and hold in front, [k2, p2] from left needle, [k2, p2] from cn, k2.

ROWS 2–8: Rep set-up row.

Rep Rows 1–8 for patt.

Cross on the Same Side

Because ribbing is reversible (with no right or wrong side), the cable crossing rows can now occur on either side. I still encourage you to work crossing rows with the same facing side every time. Designate a "front" side by marking one side (with some contrasting scrap yarn, a split-ring marker, or a plastic safety pin) or keep track of which direction the cast-on tail points. Crossing on the same side makes counting rows and keeping track of the pattern a lot easier, because you know when the crossing side faces, you are on a right-side row.

Fig. 1: Twisted rib.

Fig. 2: Tunisian crochet.

Note the differences between ribbles of 1x1 rib on page 41 and 2x2 rib (at left). 1x1 looks flatter, while 2x2 looks more puffy and three-dimensional. Because knit stitches stand out and purls recede, k2 stands out more than k1, and p2 is indented more than p1. For a bolder texture, go for the 2x2. However, note that the 2x2 cable seems less symmetrical than the 1x1; compare the right and left edges of the cable. The 2x2 rib seems more "off-kilter." The 2x2 cable begins with k2 and ends with p2, a greater difference than 1x1. Some are bothered by asymmetry, others like it. You be the judge.

Other than the visual differences between 1x1 and 2x2 ribbed cables, there is another factor that might lead you to choose one over the other. In 1x1 rib, there are more choices of how large a cable to make. In 2x2 rib, the choices for the size of cables are reduced by half! If you want more options for cable sizes, stick to 1x1 rib. It can be interesting, however, to alternate cables of each kind across a piece, creating some flatter 1x1 ribbles alongside puffier 2x2 ribbles.

You can explore further with 3x3 rib, in which each set of stitches is a multiple of 6. However, the minimum cable in 3x3 ribbing is 12 stitches (6 over 6), which limits the cable options severely. It also produces a very lopsided-looking cable, as it begins with k3 and ends with p3.

Twisted Ribs

Just as you can cable ribbing, so can you cable rib variations. One such variant rib is twisted rib. By working into the back loops of knit stitches, an almost nubby texture is achieved (Fig. 1). You can almost see little slashes of the stitches. (Ribbles in twisted rib look like Tunisian or Afghan crochet! See Fig. 2.) Be very careful of the gauge, as this stitch can be even denser than regular 1x1 ribbles. This pattern is used in the Reversible Honeycomb Scarf on page 50, which is a reversible version of the honeycomb and rope design of the Honeycomb V-neck Pullover on page 24. The scarf yarn is lighter than the pullover yarn for better drape in the denser stitch.

Fisherman's Rib

CO 17 sts.

ROW 1: (RS) Sl 1 pwise wyb, [k1, p1] to last 2 sts, k1, sl 1 pwise wyb.

ROW 2: P2, [k1 in the row below (see Glossary), p1] to last st, p1.

ROW 3: Sl 1 kwise, [k1 in the row below, p1] to last 2 sts, k1 in the row below, sl 1 pwise wyb.

Rep Rows 2 and 3 for patt.

FRONT

BACK

Half-fisherman's Rib

CO 17 sts.

ROW 1: (RS) Sl 1 pwise wyb, [k1, p1] to last 2 sts, k1, sl 1 pwise wyb.

ROW 2: P2, [k1, p1] to last st, p1.

ROW 3: Sl 1 pwise wyb, [k1 in the row below (see Glossary), p1] to last 2 sts, k1 in the row below, sl 1 pwise wyb.

Rep Rows 2 and 3 for patt.

FRONT

BACK

Fisherman's Rib

Also known as Quaker stitch, Shaker stitch, or brioche stitch, fisherman's rib (and half-fisherman's rib) is a rib variation that can be used in a reversible cable. There is also half-fisherman's rib. There are actually two ways to do this stitch: the yarnover method and working into the row below. The XOX Raglan Turtleneck on page 58 and the swatches at right use the yarnover method, while the sample at left is worked into the row below.

Fisherman's rib is spongy and spreads out. Unlike regular ribbing, this fabric does not pull in, so you see the purl areas more. Some call this a "knit twice" stitch, because the pattern uses stitches from two rows and "hikes" them up together. Like garter stitch, the stitch height is very short and compact. (In machine knitting, this type of stitch is called a tuck stitch.) The back and front are identical reversibles.

Half-fisherman's rib looks different on the front and back—they are fraternal reversibles. One side looks like regular fisherman's rib, but the other is nubby. That's because this stitch alternates one row of regular rib with one row of fisherman's rib (hence the name). The stitch height is shorter than stockinette but not as short as fisherman's rib. This does not draw in like a regular rib either, but it is not as wide as fisherman's rib.

Cables in either of these ribs are reversible, but like the uncrossed version, fisherman's rib is identical and half-fisherman's rib is fraternal.

STITCH FILE

STITCH FILE

FRONT   BACK

FRONT   BACK

Cabled Fisherman's Rib

CO 12 sts.

ROW 1: Sl 1 purlwise (pwise) with yarn in front (wyf), k1, *k1, yo, sl 1 pwise; rep from * to last 2 sts, k2.

ROW 2: Sl 1 pwise wyf, k1, *knit next st tog with yo above it, yo, sl 1 pwise; rep from * to last 2 sts, k2.

Rep Row 2 for patt.

Cabled Half-fisherman's Rib

CO 12 sts.

ROW 1: (WS) Sl 1 pwise wyf, k1, *k1, yo, sl 1 pwise; rep from * to last 2 sts, k2.

ROW 2: Sl 1 pwise wyf, k1, *knit next st tog with yo above it, p1; rep from * to last 2 sts, k2.

Rep Rows 1 and 2 for patt.

GAUGE CONSIDERATIONS

Ribbing and cables both draw in, so using both ribs and cables really thickens up the fabric. To avoid fabric as stiff and thick as cardboard, you will probably want to go up in needle size. The number of needle sizes to go up depends on the yarn as well as the project. Try swatches in a few needle sizes to arrive at your own personal preference. On the other hand, some projects benefit from being worked firmly. If you continued to work the patterns on page 45, you'd make a belt, which should be firm since it gets tugged on a lot.

Those patterns begin with about an inch of ribbing with garter stitches on each side, which establishes the rib pattern and keeps the bottom edge from puckering and waving. See how the bottom rib flares? That's because the cables draw in even more than ribbing alone. To compensate, work that initial inch in a needle size similar to the one you'd use for stockinette stitch with the given yarn, then switch to larger needles when the cabling begins. After the last cabling row of the project, change back to the smaller needles and work ribbing for about an inch, then bind off very tightly. This will prevent flared bottoms (and who among us likes flared bottoms?).

Preferred Fibers

Some yarns take better to a looser gauge than others. Lofty yarns work best for this technique; I prefer yarns with some mohair content, but angora or brushed wool or alpaca yarns work well, too. If you can't wear any animal fibers, even brushed acrylics might do the job. The fuzz from a lofty, haloed yarn covers up the gaping spaces of a loosened gauge. Just make sure the yarn is not so hairy that it covers up the stitch textures.

This is not to say that ribbles cannot be successful in denser fibers such as cotton or silk; they're just trickier and less expandable. I generally go up two to three needle sizes over the ball band suggestion in loftier yarns, but I go up only one to two needle sizes with denser yarns.

CHARTING REVERSIBLE CABLES

What about expressing cables on paper? Charts usually show us what the cable looks like on the right side, but what about when there's no wrong side? Try our old visualization exercise: With the palm of your right hand facing downward and the middle finger crossed over the index finger, the top or middle finger slants left (a left cross). Keeping your fingers crossed, look at the palm side. The top finger (which is now the index finger) still slants left. The finger that was on the bottom slanting right is now on top slanting left. Conversely, the finger that used to be on top slanting left is now on the bottom slanting right. Although

Fig. 1: Reversible "cables," front.

the finger on top changes, a left cross shows on either side.

This visualization works for the basic rope cable, where you are always crossing the same stitches in the same direction. But what happens in a more complex cable where both directions of cables are in use, such as a staghorn or V cable? Most of us have only two hands! Short of working a swatch, how do you know what the other side will look like in a reversibly cabled piece with cables crossing in different directions? In my classes, I have students stand up with their arms crossed in the air to demonstrate. You can get a bunch of friends to line up together to do this pantomime, but it's cumbersome.

As pictured, the guy (on the right) is a right cross and the gal (on the left) is a left cross (**Fig. 1**). This combination forms a "V" from the front. View them both on from back, however, and they form an upside-down "V" or a wishbone. On the back, the left-cross gal comes first (on the right) and the right-cross guy comes (later on the left; **Fig. 2**).

This is where your movement charts (see page 13) really come in handy. Notice how, on one side, the line indicating the stitches that wind up on the bottom gets "broken" in the middle. On the back, these bottom stitches wind up on top. If we were to draw the back, it would become the solid line, while the solid line of the front becomes the broken line. But does it go right or left?

You need to see the back and the front to know what the finished cable will look like. Gridded tracing paper (available at most art supply stores) or magic markers that show through regular graph paper come in handy. After charting your pattern, label it "front," then turn the paper over (**Fig. 3**). Label another piece of paper "back" and redraw your pattern, drawing all lines in the same directions but making the broken lines solid and breaking the solid lines (**Fig. 4**). In other words, don't reverse directions, just reverse the broken-ness. (See figures 3a and 3b, next page.)

Truth be told, I chart on a computer these days. To chart the back, I flip the image horizontally, then redraw the "overs" and "unders" (the broken lines and the solid lines).

Fig. 3: "V."   Fig. 4: Upside down "V."

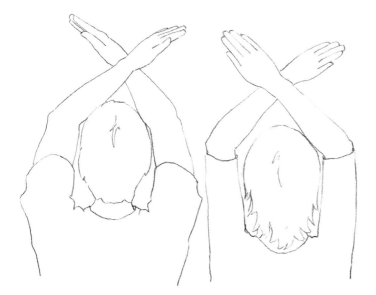

Fig. 2: Reversible "cables," back.

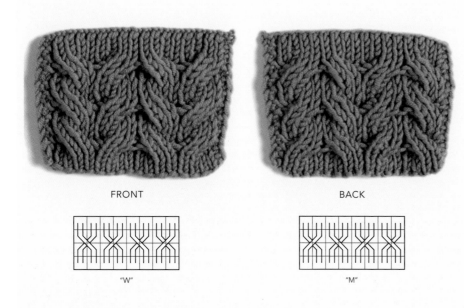

FRONT

BACK

"W"

"M"

Reversible Staghorn

With smaller needles, CO 36 sts.

SET-UP ROW: Sl 1 pwise wyf, k1, [k1, p1] 16 times, k2.

Rep last row until piece measures about 1" (2.5 cm).

ROW 1: (cable row) With larger needles, sl 1 pwise wyf, k1, *sl 4 sts to cn and hold in back, [k1, p1, k1, p1] from left needle, [k1, p1, k1, p1] from cn, sl 4 sts to cn and hold in front, [k1, p1, k1, p1] from left needle, [k1, p1, k1, p1] from cn; rep from * once, k2.

ROWS 2–6: Rep set-up row.

Rep Rows 1–6 for patt, ending after Row 1.

NEXT ROW: With smaller needles, rep set-up row.

Rep last row for about 1" (2.5 cm). BO all sts.

REVERSIBILITY IN ACTION

Consider the Staghorn cable again. This is just two rope cables side by side; the first is a right cross and the next is a left cross. After charting and redrawing, you can see that the staghorn turns upside down (or becomes a wishbone) instead of a V. Add a repeat of another four sets of stitches (or another pair of rope cables), and the front shows a W while the back becomes an M. Knit a swatch to see for yourself how recharting and redrawing work (and changing needle sizes to prevent flaring, too).

With a braid cable worked in reversible ribs, the backs of the cables **(Fig. 5b)** will differ somewhat from the fronts **(Fig. 5a)**. Again, you can see the difference by charting the front, reversing the tracing paper for the back, and

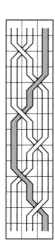

Fig. 5a: Braid front.

Fig. 5b: Braid back.

Fig 6a: Honeycomb front.

Fig. 6b: Honeycomb back.

redrawing. The pattern on the back of the braid cable turns upside down. For honeycomb lozenges, the pattern in front is the opposite on back: Where the cables pull outward from the "front," **(Fig. 6a)** they come together inward from the "back," and vice versa **(Fig. 6b)**. The difference may be negligible; the final effect in either case is a series of lozenges atop one another.

Borders and Separators

In the Stitch Files in this chapter, the side borders have been knitted as you go and not worked afterward. If borders were added afterward by picking up stitches along the edges, the pick-up row would create a ridge, which would keep the piece from being truly reversible. To avoid this problem, add 2 to 4 stitches on each side (usually in garter stitch) to frame the sides. For the top and bottom borders, work ribbing on needles smaller than the ones to be used for the main portion, and

Fig. 7: Cables separated by reversible separator stitches.

bind off tightly.

For standard (non-reversible) cables, it's typical to have purl stitches on each side to accentuate the cable. But in a reversible piece, the purl stitches become knit stitches. Instead of reverse stockinette, use a reversible stitch such as garter or seed stitch (or even more ribbing) as separator or filler stitches **(Fig. 7)**.

APPLICATIONS

Besides the ubiquitous scarf or shawl or afghan, what other projects benefit from being reversible? Anything that flips over or turns back: belts, straps for handbags, hoods, socks (such as the ones on page 54), turtlenecks (see page 58), or stoles (see page 118).

Reversibility often means versatility. Different wearing options can extend your wardrobe. Sleeve cuffs can be folded back to three-quarter length or down for a full sleeve. Reversibility also extends function; if it's too warm, fold back a lapel or collar or turn up the hat brim. When it's chilly, put up a turtleneck or pull down a mitten cuff.

There are enough combination and variation possibilities here to keep you experimenting for a very, very long time. Most importantly, cables that were formerly unappealing from the "wrong" side need never be so ever again, and there is nothing to deter you from incorporating them into scarves, shawls, afghans, collars, lapels—any place where reversibility is a plus.

REVERSIBLE
honeycomb scarf

This reversible scarf includes the same honeycomb and rope cable patterns as the V-Neck Pullover on page 24 but is worked reversibly. The scarf is worked in a thinner yarn for more drape and detail, and the twisted ribs offer even more texture. Make this alone or as a companion piece to the Honeycomb Pullover.

FINISHED MEASUREMENTS
7" (18 cm) wide and 57" (145 cm) long.

YARN
DK weight (Light #3).
Shown here: Mission Falls 136 Wool (100% superwash merino, 136 yd [124 m]/50 g): Pistachio #028, 6 skeins.

NEEDLES
U.S. sizes 5 (3.75 mm) and 8 (5 mm). Adjust needle sizes if necessary to obtain the correct gauge.

NOTIONS
Stitch markers (m); cable needle (cn); tapestry needle.

GAUGE
34-st center panel = 3½" (9.5 cm).
18-st side panel = 1¾" (4.5 cm).
30 rows = 4" (10 cm) in all patterns.

NOTES

Markers denote side patterns and center panel; slip markers (sl m) as you come to them.
Needles used are much larger than normally used for this weight of yarn to prevent excessively dense fabric.
Although there is no true "wrong" side, the sides are designated as RS and WS for clarification.

stitch guide

Twisted Rib (multiple of 2 sts + 1): All rows: [K1tbl, p1] to last st, k1tbl.

4/4RRC (4 over 4 Ribbed Right Cross): Sl 4 sts to cn and hold in back, work 4 sts from left needle in Twisted Rib, work 4 sts from cn in Twisted Rib.

4/4RLC (4 over 4 Ribbed Left Cross): Sl 4 sts to cn and hold in front, work 4 sts from left needle in Twisted Rib, work 4 sts from cn in Twisted Rib.

8/8RRC (8 over 8 Ribbed Right Cross): Sl 8 sts to cn and hold in back, work 8 sts from left needle in Twisted Rib, work 8 sts from cn in Twisted Rib.

8/8RLC (8 over 8 Ribbed Left Cross): Sl 8 sts to cn and hold in front, work 8 sts from left needle in Twisted Rib, work 8 sts from cn in Twisted Rib.

Right Ribbed Rope (18 sts)

ROW 1: (RS) K1, 8/8RRC, k1.

ROWS 2–16: K1, *k1tbl, p1; rep from * to last st, k1.

Rep Rows 1–16 for patt.

Left Ribbed Rope (18 sts)

ROW 1: (RS) K1, 8/8LRC, k1.

ROWS 2–16: K1, *k1tbl, p1; rep from * to last st, k1.

Rep Rows 1–16 for patt.

Honeycomb (34 sts)

ROW 1: (RS) K1, [4/4RRC, 4/4RLC] twice, k1.

ROWS 2–12: K1, [k1tbl, p1] 16 times, k1.

ROW 13: K1, [4/4RLC, 4/4RRC] twice, k1.

ROWS 14–24: K1, [k1tbl, p1] 16 times, k1.

Rep Rows 1–24 for patt.

SCARF

With smaller needles, CO 72 sts.

Bottom Border

Border patt: Sl 1 purlwise (pwise) with yarn in front (wyf), k1, [k1tbl, p1] 8 times, k1, place marker (pm), k1, [k1tbl, p1] 16 times, k1, pm, k1, [k1tbl, p1] 8 times, k2. Rep border patt each row, until piece measures 1" (2.5 cm).

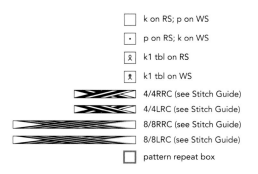

☐ k on RS; p on WS

· p on RS; k on WS

k1 tbl on RS

k1 tbl on WS

4/4RRC (see Stitch Guide)

4/4LRC (see Stitch Guide)

8/8RRC (see Stitch Guide)

8/8LRC (see Stitch Guide)

☐ pattern repeat box

Left Ribbed Rope

16 sts

Main Body

Next row: With larger needles, sl 1 pwise wyf, work Right Ribbed Rope patt to m, work Honeycomb to next m, work Left Ribbed Rope patt to last st, k1.

Next row: Sl 1, pwise wyf, work Left Ribbed Rope patt to m, work Honeycomb to next m, work Right Ribbed Rope patt to last st, k1.

Continue in patt as established, beg all rows with sl 1 pwise wyf and ending all rows with k1, until piece measures 56" (142 cm), ending after Row 1 of Ribbed Rope patterns.

Top Border

With smaller needles, work Border patt for 1" (2.5 cm). BO very tightly in patt on next row.

Finishing

Block piece to measurements. Weave in ends.

Honeycomb

23 21 19 17 15 13 11 9 7 5 3 1

Right Ribbed Rope

15 13 11 9 7 5 3 1

32 sts

16 sts

REVERSIBLE-CUFF
cabled socks

The reversible cables in these socks allow the cuffs to be worn up over the ankle or turned down as ankle socks. The reversible cables also mean that you can wear the socks turned inside out, should you not have the time to do laundry! Note that the patterns of each sock are mirror images of each other.

FINISHED SIZES

5¾ (7¾, 9¾, 11¾, 13½)" (14.5 [19.5, 25, 30, 34.5] cm) foot circumference. Socks shown measure 7¾" (19 cm).

YARN

Fingering (Super Fine #1).
Shown here: Crystal Palace Panda Silk (52% bamboo, 43% superwash merino, 5% silk; 204 yd [187 m]/50 g): Berry Smoothie #3006, 1 (2, 2, 2, 3) skeins.

NEEDLES

U.S. sizes 1 (2.25 mm) and 3 (3.25 mm): set of 4 double-pointed (dpn). Adjust needle sizes if necessary to obtain the correct gauge.

NOTIONS

Cable needle (cn); tapestry needle.

GAUGE

41 sts and 38 rnds = 4" (10 cm) in Ribbed Cable patt on larger needles.
34 sts and 48 rnds = 4" (10 cm) in St st on smaller needles.

NOTE

Socks are mirror images of each other. Work Ribbed Cable A for first sock and Ribbed Cable B for second sock.

stitch guide

2/2RRC (2 over 2 ribbed right cross): Sl 2 sts to cn and hold in back of work, [k1, p1, k1, p1] from left needle, [k1, p1, k1, p1] from cn.

2/2RLC (2 over 2 ribbed left cross): Sl 2 sts to cn and hold in front of work, [k1, p1, k1, p1] from left needle, [k1, p1, k1, p1] from cn.

Ribbed Cable Pattern A: (multiple of 8 sts)

RND 1: *2/2RRC, [k1, p1] 2 times; rep from * to end.

RNDS 2–6: [K1, p1] to end.

RNDS 7–12: Rep Rnds 1–6.

RND 13: *[k1, p1] 2 times, 2/2RRC; rep from * to end.

RNDS 14–18: [K1, p1] to end.

RNDS 19–24: Rep Rnds 13–18.

Rep Rnds 1–24 for patt.

Ribbed Cable Pattern B: (multiple of 8 sts)

RND 1: *[K1, p1] 2 times, 2/2RLC; rep from * to end.

RNDS 2–6: [K1, p1] to end.

RNDS 7–12: Rep Rnds 1–6.

RND 13: *2/2RLC, [k1, p1] 2 times; rep from * to end.

RNDS 14–18: [K1, p1] to end.

RNDS 19–24: Rep Rnds 13–18.

Rep Rnds 1–24 for patt.

Ribbed Cable A

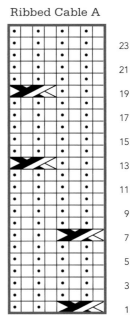

Ribbed Cable B

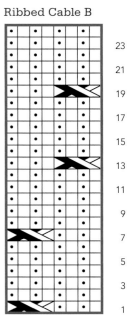

☐ k

• p

2/2RRC (see Stitch Guide)

2/2LRC (see Stitch Guide)

☐ pattern repeat box

SOCK

Cuff

With larger dpns, CO 48 (64, 80, 96, 112) sts. Arrange as evenly as possible on 3 dpns and join for working in the rnd, being careful not to twist sts. Beg Ribbed Cable Patt (A for first sock, B for second).
  Work Ribbed Cable Patt until cuff measures 5½" (14 cm) or desired length to ankle. Change to smaller dpns and work in St st for ½" (1.3 cm).

Short-row Heel

Arrange sts as foll: Needle 1—24 (32, 40, 48, 56) sts; Needle 2—12 (16, 20, 24, 28) sts; Needle 3—12 (16, 20, 24, 28) sts. Heel is worked back and forth with short-rows (see Glossary) on Needle 1.

Short-row 1: (RS) Knit to last st of Needle 1, wrap & turn (w & t; see Glossary).

Short-row 2: Purl to last st, w & t.

Short-row 3: Knit to last unwrapped st, w & t.

Short-row 4: Purl to last unwrapped st, w & t.

Rep Short-rows 3 and 4 [7 (10, 12, 15, 17)] times; 8 (10, 14, 16, 20) sts rem between wraps on last WS row, w & t.

Next row: (RS) K8 (10, 14, 16, 20), work each wrap tog with wrapped sts to end of needle, wrap first st on Needle 2, return wrapped st to Needle 2 and turn.

Next row: Purl to next wrapped st, work each wrap tog with wrapped sts to end of needle, wrap first st on Needle 3, return wrapped st to Needle 3 and turn.

Short-row 1: (RS) K16 (21, 27, 32, 38), w & t.

Short-row 2: P8 (10, 14, 16, 20), w & t.

Short-row 3: Knit to last wrapped st, work wrap tog with wrapped st, w & t.

Short-row 4: Purl to last wrapped st, work wrap tog with wrapped st, w & t.

Rep last 2 rows until last st on WS row has been wrapped.

Next row: Needle 1—work wrap tog with wrapped st, knit to last st on needle, work wrap tog with wrapped st; Needle 2—work wrap tog with wrapped st, knit to end of needle; Needle 3—knit to last st on needle, then work wrap tog with wrapped st.
  Resume working in the rnd.

Foot

Work in St st until sock is 2" (5 cm) shorter than desired foot length measured from back of heel (or about to tip of little toe).

Toe

Set-up row: Needle 1—knit; Needle 2—knit. Beg of Needle 3 is new beg of rnd; beg of rnds is now at top of foot and Needle 3 becomes Needle 1.

Rnd 1: Needle 1—knit to last 3 sts, k2tog, k1; Needle 2—k1, ssk, knit to last 3 sts, k2tog, k1; Needle 3—k1, ssk, knit to end—4 sts dec'd.

Rnd 2: Knit.

Rep Rnds 1 and 2 [7 (10, 13, 16, 19) times]—16 (20, 24, 28, 32) sts remain. With Needle 3, k4 (5, 6, 7, 8) sts from Needle 1—8 (10, 12, 14. 16) sts on each of 2 dpns. Cut yarn, leaving an 8" (20.5 cm) tail.

With tail threaded on tapestry needle, use Kitchener st (see Glossary) to graft sts tog. (If you prefer, you may work a 3-needle BO; see Glossary.)

XOX RAGLAN
turtleneck

The A-line silhouette of this tunic shapes itself—the number of stitches remains the same, but each of the three stitch patterns has a different stitch gauge, with the widest on bottom and the narrowest on top. The Half-fisherman's Rib of the turtleneck creates a fraternal reversible pattern. Wear the turtleneck up in cooler weather and turn it down indoors or in warmer weather.

FINISHED MEASUREMENTS

35 (38, 41, 44, 47)" (89 [96.5, 104, 112, 119.5] cm) bust circumference and 25½ (26, 26, 26½, 26½)" (65 [66, 66, 67.5, 67.5] cm) long; to be worn with average ease. Sweater shown measures 38" (96.5 cm).

YARN

DK weight (Light #3).
Shown here: Zitron Ecco (100% superwash merino; 120 yd [110 m]/50 g): beige #112, 13 (14, 15, 16, 17) skeins.

NEEDLES

U.S. size 7 (4.5 mm): straight and 16" (40 cm) circular (cir). Adjust needle size if necessary to obtain the correct gauge.

NOTIONS

Stitch markers (m); cable needle (cn); tapestry needle.

GAUGE

23 sts and 32 rows = 4" (10 cm) in beaded rib.
22 sts and 40 rows = 4" (10 cm) in half-fisherman's rib.
20 sts and 50 rows = 4" (10 cm) in fisherman's rib.
Center cable panel = 2" (5 cm) in beaded rib, 2½" (6.5 cm) in half-fisherman's rib, and 2¾" (7 cm) in fisherman's rib.

NOTES

Since the neck portion is reversible, use the Russian join (see Glossary) to attach new yarn balls there if necessary.
Markers indicate garter st side borders; slip markers (sl m) as you come to them.
All sl sts are worked purlwise (pwise) with yarn in back (wyb) except for ssk and ssp decreases, in which sts are slipped knitwise.
Cables are generally crossed every 16th row in fisherman's rib, every 12th row in half-fisherman's rib, and every 8th row in beaded rib.
Cables in the neck portion should continue crossing as closely as possible to the cables at the center of the front to continue the XOX pattern into the neck portion. If possible, end front before beginning to shape the neck about 2 rows after crossing a cable.

stitch guide

Fisherman's Rib

ROW 1: (RS; set-up row) Sl 1, *k1, yo, sl 1; rep from * to last 2 sts, k1, sl 1.

ROW 2: (WS) P1, sl 1, yo, *knit next st tog with the yo above it, yo, sl 1; rep from * to last st, p1.

ROW 3: Sl 1, *knit next st tog with the yo above it, yo, sl 1; rep from * to last 2 sts, knit next st tog with the yo above it, sl 1.

Rep Rows 2 and 3 for patt.

Half-fisherman's Rib

ROW 1: (RS) Sl 1, *knit next st tog with the yo above it, p1; rep from * to last 2 sts, knit next st tog with the yo above it, sl 1.

ROW 2: (WS) P1, *yo, sl 1, p1; rep from * to end.

Rep Rows 1 and 2 for patt.

Beaded Rib

ROW 1: (RS; transition row) Sl 1, *knit next st tog with the yo above it, k1; rep from * to last 2 sts, knit next st tog with the yo above it, sl 1.

ROW 2: (WS) P2, * k1, p1; rep from * to last st, p1.

ROW 3: (RS) Knit.

Rep Rows 2 and 3 for patt.

4/4RC (4 over 4 Right Cross): Sl next 4 sts to cn and hold in back, work 4 sts from left needle in patt, work 4 sts from cn in patt.

4/4LC (4 over 4 Left Cross): Sl next 4 sts to cn and hold in front, work 4 sts from left needle in patt, work 4 sts from cn in patt.

Cable in Fisherman's Rib (over center 17 sts)

ROWS 1–4: Work in Fisherman's Rib patt.

ROW 5: 4/4RC (will look like 6 sts on cn because of yos above first and third sts), knit next (center) st tog with the yo above it, 4/4LC (will look like 6 sts on cn because of yos above second and fourth sts).

ROWS 6–20: Work in Fisherman's Rib patt as established.

ROW 21: 4/4LC, knit next (center) st tog with the yo above it, 4/4RC (see notes on Row 5 regarding stitch counts).

ROWS 22–36: Work in Fisherman's Rib patt as established.

ROW 37: Rep Row 21.

ROWS 38–52: Work in Fisherman's Rib patt as established.

ROW 53: Rep Row 5.

ROWS 54–65: Work in Fisherman's Rib patt as established.

Rep Rows 2–65 for patt.

Cable in Half-fisherman's Rib (over center 17 sts)

ROWS 1–6: Work Half-fisherman's Rib patt.

ROW 7: 4/4RC (will look like 6 sts on cn because of yos above first and third sts), knit next (center) st tog with the yo above it, 4/4LC (will look like 6 sts on cn because of yos above second and fourth sts).

ROWS 8–18: Work Half-fisherman's Rib patt as established.

ROW 19: Rep Row 7.

ROWS 20–30: Work Half-fisherman's Rib patt as established.

ROW 31: 4/4LC, knit next (center) st tog with the yo above it, 4/4RC (see notes on Row 7 regarding stitch counts).

ROWS 32–42: Work Half-fisherman's Rib patt as established.

ROW 43: Rep Row 31.

ROWS 44–48: Work Half-fisherman's Rib patt as established.

Rep Rows 1–48 for patt.

Cable in Beaded Rib (over center 17 sts)

ROW 1: (RS; transition row) Sl 1, *knit next st tog with the yo above it, k1; rep from * to last 2 sts, knit next st tog with the yo above it, sl 1.

ROWS 2–6: Work Beaded Rib patt.

ROW 7: 4/4LC, k1, 4/4RC.

ROWS 8–14: Work in Beaded Rib patt as established.

ROW 15: 4/4RC, k1, 4/4LC.

ROWS 16–22: Work in Beaded Rib patt as established.

ROW 23: Rep Row 15.

ROWS 24–30: Work in Beaded Rib patt as established.

ROW 31: Rep Row 7.

ROWS 32 AND 33: Work in Beaded Rib patt as established.

Rep Rows 2–33 for patt.

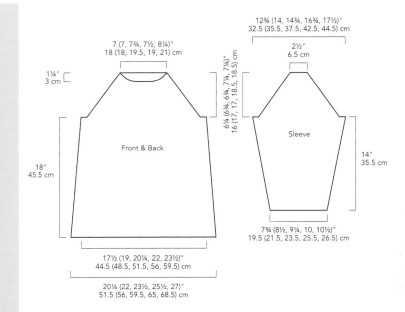

12¾ (14, 14¾, 16¾, 17½)"
32.5 (35.5, 37.5, 42.5, 44.5) cm

7 (7, 7¾, 7½, 8¼)"
18 (18, 19.5, 19, 21) cm

2½"
6.5 cm

1¼"
3 cm

6¼ (6¾, 6¾, 7¼, 7¼)"
16 (17, 17, 18.5, 18.5) cm

Front & Back

Sleeve

18"
45.5 cm

14"
35.5 cm

17½ (19, 20¼, 22, 23½)"
44.5 (48.5, 51.5, 56, 59.5) cm

20¼ (22, 23½, 25½, 27)"
51.5 (56, 59.5, 65, 68.5) cm

7¾ (8½, 9¼, 10, 10½)"
19.5 (21.5, 23.5, 25.5, 26.5) cm

Fisherman's Rib & Cable

Half-Fisherman's Rib & Cable

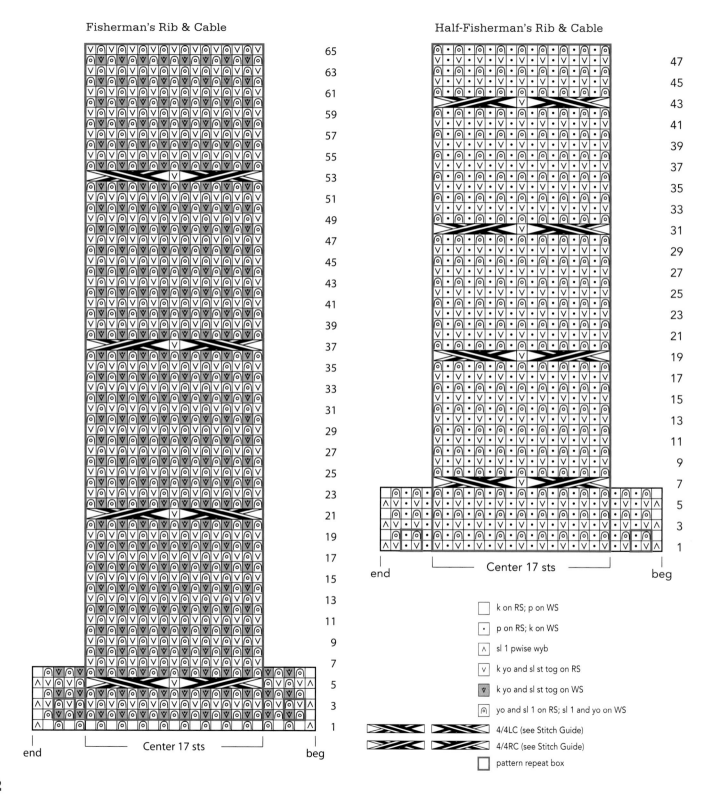

| k on RS; p on WS |
•	p on RS; k on WS
∧	sl 1 pwise wyb
v	k yo and sl st tog on RS
v	k yo and sl st tog on WS
⍴	yo and sl 1 on RS; sl 1 and yo on WS
4/4LC (see Stitch Guide)
4/4RC (see Stitch Guide)
pattern repeat box

Beaded Rib & Cable

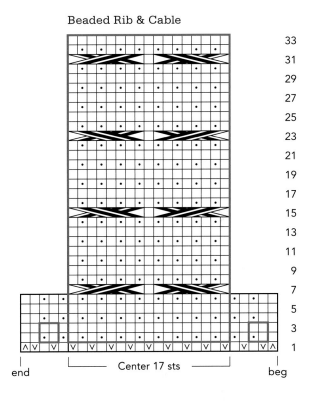

BACK

Using the crochet or chain method (see Glossary), very loosely CO 103 (111, 119, 129, 137) sts.

Work Fisherman's Rib patt until piece measures 8½" (21.5 cm), ending after a WS row.

Work Half-fisherman's Rib patt until piece measures 17" (43 cm), ending after a WS row.

Work Beaded Rib patt until piece measures 18" (45.5 cm), ending after a WS row.

Shape Armholes

Next row: (RS; BO row) BO 5 (6, 7, 9, 11) sts, k2, work in patt to end—98 (105, 112, 120, 126) sts rem.

Next row: (WS; BO row) BO 5 (6, 7, 9, 11) sts, p2, work in patt to end—93 (99, 105, 111, 115) sts.

Next row: (RS; dec row) Continuing in patt as established (Beaded Rib patt with selvedge of 2 St sts each end), k1, k2tog, work in patt to last 3 sts, ssk, k1—2 sts dec'd; 91 (97, 103, 109, 113) sts rem.

Next row: Work even in patt as established.

Rep last 2 rows 20 (21, 20, 20, 20) more times, then rep dec row once more—49 (53, 61, 67, 71) sts rem.

Next row: (WS; dec row) P1, ssp, work in patt to last 3 sts, p2tog, p1—47 (51, 59, 65, 69) sts rem.

Rep last 2 dec rows 1 (2, 3, 5, 5) more times—43 (43, 47, 45, 49) sts rem.

BO all sts kwise.

FRONT

Using the crochet or chain method, very loosely CO 107 (115, 123, 135, 143) sts.

Row 1: Work Row 1 of Fisherman's Rib patt for 44 (49, 53, 59, 63) sts, place marker (pm), work Row 1 of Cable patt in Fisherman's Rib for 17 sts, pm, work Row 1 of Fisherman's Rib patt to end. Work Fisherman's Rib patt over left and right sides and Cable patt in Fisherman's Rib over center 17 sts until piece measures 8½" (21.5 cm), ending after a WS row.

Work Half-fisherman's Rib patt over left and right sides and Cable patt in Half-fisherman's Rib over center 17 sts until piece measures 17" (43 cm), ending after a WS row.

Begin Beaded Rib patt over left and right sides and Cable patt in Beaded Rib over center 17 sts until piece measures 18" (45.5 cm), ending after a WS row.

Shape Armholes

Work armhole shaping as for Back until armhole measures 4½" (5", 5", 5½", 5½") (11.5 [12.5, 12.5, 14, 14] cm), ending after a RS row—63 (65, 71, 75, 79) sts. Mark center 29 (29, 31, 31, 33) sts for neck.

Shape Neck

Next row: (WS; BO row) Continuing to work armhole shaping as for back, work in patt to m, join second ball of yarn and BO center 29 (29, 31, 31, 33) sts, work in patt to end.

Working each side of front separately, continue decreases as established at each armhole edge, and BO 2 (2, 3, 3, 4) sts at each neck edge one time, then dec 1 st at each neck edge on next RS row as foll: work in patt to last 3 sts of left front, ssk, k1; at beg of right front k1, k2tog, work in patt to end. Work dec at each neck edge in this manner every RS row 4 more times. Bind off rem 2 sts kwise on next RS row.

The turtleneck, worked in Half-fisherman's Rib, is a fraternal reversible (shown from the outside of the sweater at left and the inside at right).

SLEEVES

Using the crochet or chain method, very loosely CO 51 (55, 59, 63, 67) sts.

Row 1: (WS) Work Row 21 of Beaded Rib patt for 17 (19, 21, 23, 25) sts, pm, work Row 2 of Cable patt in Beaded Rib for 17 sts, pm, work Row 2 of Beaded Rib patt to end.

Rows 2–6 (6, 6, 4, 4): Work Beaded Rib patt over left and right sides and Cable patt in Beaded Rib.

Next row: (RS; inc row) K2, M1 (see Glossary), work in patt to last 2 sts, M1, k2—53 (57, 61, 65, 69) sts.

Continuing in patt as established (Beaded Rib patt on left and right sides, Cable patt in Beaded Rib on center sts, and selvedge of 2 St sts each end), rep inc row every 6th row 0 (0, 0, 16, 16) more times, then every 8th row 7 (15, 15, 3, 3) times, then every 10th row 6 (0, 0, 0, 0) times; work new sts in Beaded Rib patt—79 (87, 91, 103, 107) sts.

Work even in patt until piece measures 14" (35.5 cm), ending after a WS row.

Raglan Shaping

Next row: (RS; BO row) BO 5 (6, 7, 9, 11) sts, k2, work in patt to end—74 (81, 84, 94, 96) sts rem.

Next row: (WS; BO row) BO 5 (6, 7, 9, 11) sts, p2, work in patt to end—69 (75, 77, 85, 85) sts.

Next row: (RS; dec row) Continuing in patt as established (Beaded Rib patt with selvedge of 2 St sts each end), k1, k2tog, work in patt to last 3 sts, ssk, k1—2 sts dec'd; 67 (73, 75, 83, 83) sts rem.

Next row: Work even in patt as established.

Rep last 2 rows 20 (21, 20, 20, 20) more times, then rep dec row one more time—25 (29, 33, 41, 41) sts rem.

Next row: (WS; dec row) P1, ssp, work in patt to last 3 sts, p2tog, p1—23 (27, 31, 39, 39) sts rem.

Rep last 2 dec rows 1 (2, 3, 5, 5) more times—19 sts rem. BO all sts kwise.

FINISHING

Block pieces to measurements. With yarn threaded on a tapestry needle, sew sleeve, underarm, and side.

Turtleneck

With RS facing, cir needle, and beg at center Back Neck st, pick up and knit (see Glossary) 19 (19, 19, 22, 22) sts evenly to back shoulder seam, 17 sts across left sleeve, 19 (19, 19, 23, 23) sts evenly along left front neck to Center Cable, 17 sts along Center Cable, 19 (19, 19, 23, 23) sts evenly along right front neck to front shoulder seam, 17 sts across right sleeve, 18 (18, 18, 21, 21) sts evenly to center back neck—126 (126, 126, 140, 140) sts. Pm for beg of rnd and join for working in the rnd.

SIZES 35 (38, 41)" ONLY

Rnd 1: (set-up rnd) [P1, k1] to end.

Rnd 2: [Yo, sl 1, k1] to end.

Rnd 3: [Purl next st tog with the yo above it, k1] to end.

Rnds 4–6: Rep Rnds 2 and 3.

Rnd 7: *P1, work next appropriate cable crossing over next 17 sts; rep from * to end.

Rnds 8–18: Rep Rnds 2 and 3.

Rnd 19: *P1, work cable over next 17 sts; rep from * to end.

Rnds 20–30: Rep Rnds 2 and 3.

Rnd 31: *P1, work next cable crossing over next 17 sts; rep from * to end.

Rnds 32–42: Rep Rnds 2 and 3.

Rnd 43: *P1, work next cable crossing over next 17 sts; rep from * to end.

Rnds 44 and 45: Rep Rnds 2 and 3.

BO all sts loosely in k1, p1 rib.

SIZES 44 (47)" ONLY

Rnd 1: (set-up rnd) [k1, p1] to end.

Rnd 2: [K1, yo, sl 1] to end.

Rnd 3: [K1, purl next st tog with the yo above it] to end.

Rnds 4–6: Rep Rnds 2 and 3.

Rnd 7: *K1, p1, work next cable crossing over next 17 sts, p1; rep from * to end.

Rnds 8–18: Rep Rnds 2 and 3.

Rnd 19: *K1, p1, work next cable crossing over next 17 sts, p1; rep from * to end.

Rnds 20–30: Rep Rnds 2 and 3.

Rnd 31: *K1, p1, work next cable crossing over next 17 sts, p1; rep from * to end.

Rnds 32–42: Rep Rnds 2 and 3.

Rnd 43: *K1, p1, work next cable crossing over next 17 sts, p1; rep from * to end.

Rnds 44 and 45: Rep Rnds 2 and 3.

BO all sts loosely in k1, p1 rib.

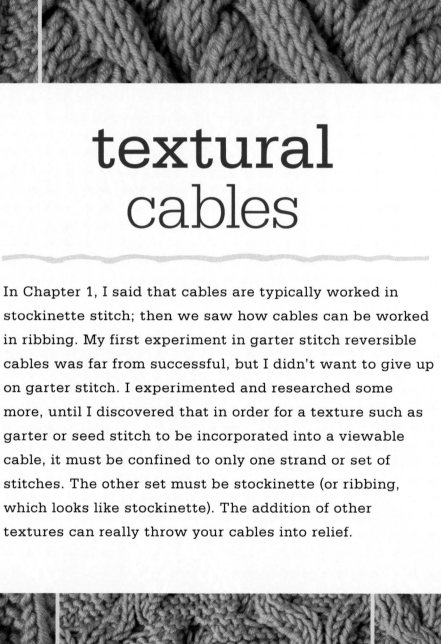

textural
cables

In Chapter 1, I said that cables are typically worked in stockinette stitch; then we saw how cables can be worked in ribbing. My first experiment in garter stitch reversible cables was far from successful, but I didn't want to give up on garter stitch. I experimented and researched some more, until I discovered that in order for a texture such as garter or seed stitch to be incorporated into a viewable cable, it must be confined to only one strand or set of stitches. The other set must be stockinette (or ribbing, which looks like stockinette). The addition of other textures can really throw your cables into relief.

CONTRASTING CABLES

In the simple rope cables at right, a different texture snakes its way around the stockinette or rib strand. In order to work, there needs to be contrast between smooth and textured strands. Alternating textures not only emphasize movement, they also add another layer or dimension. Try reverse stockinette crossed over stockinette. In the Textured Tote on page 74, cables of garter and stockinette stitches create a gnarly effect.

The swatches at right show the front of two different cable pairings: near right, stockinette crossed with seed stitch (**Fig. 1a**), and far right, ribbing crossed with garter stitch (**Fig. 2a**).

Reversibility

Both garter and seed are reversible stitches. Either one combined with stockinette in a cable creates a somewhat reversible cable. When either texture is combined with ribbing in a cable, the resulting cable is fully reversible. The back of the swatches at right demonstrates how the stitches used determine whether a textured cable is reversible. The cable is hard to see in the stockinette/seed example (**Fig. 1b**), but the ribbing/garter swatch is an identical reversible (**Fig. 2b**). In the Staghorn Cabled Coat on page 78, the lapels and cuffs fold back for different looks.

Figs. 1a and 1b: The cable crosses seed stitch with stockinette (shown front and back).

Figs. 2a and 2b: The cable crosses garter stitch with ribbing (shown front and back).

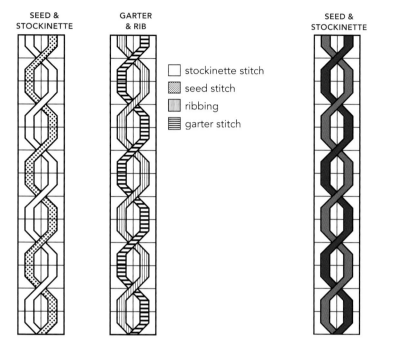

Fig. 3: Charts of cables shown in Figure 1.

Fig. 4: Colored-in strands indicate strands worked in different textures.

Legend (Fig. 3):
☐ stockinette stitch
▨ seed stitch
▥ ribbing
▤ garter stitch

Legend (Fig. 4):
■ stockinette stitch
■ seed stitch
■ ribbing
■ garter stitch

CHARTING COMBINATIONS

Charting different stitches in cables is the same as for other cables, except that garter stitch is indicated with little horizontal lines and seed stitch shown with dotted lines. Use vertical lines to indicate ribbing. Dotted and horizontal lines can be broken just as the solid lines were to represent crossing direction (**Fig. 3**). Another option is to use different-colored pencils or markers. Orange can represent garter, blue can be stockinette, green can be seed stitch, and red can mean ribbing (**Fig. 4**).

To view the back of a textured reversible cable, use tracing paper and flip the paper over (see page 47) (**Fig. 5**). Where there were broken patterns on the front, they will be uninterrupted on the back (and vice versa), so adjust accordingly. The only difference between the front and back is that the textures are opposite. Seed stitch is on top after the first crossing on one side, but stockinette is on top after this first crossing on the other side. Stockinette is on top after the second crossing on one side, but seed stitch is on top after the second crossing on the other side.

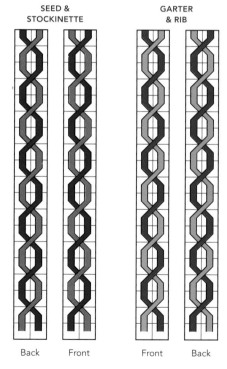

Fig. 5: Fronts and backs of the cables shown in Figure 3.

STITCH FILE

Sand Cable in Stockinette Stitch

CO 10 sets of sts.

*Work in St st to first crossing row.

FIRST CROSSING ROW: [Knit 2 sets without crossing, work Left Cross] 2 times, knit 2 sets without crossing.

Work in St st to second crossing row.

SECOND CROSSING ROW: [Work Right Cross, knit 2 sets without crossing] 2 times, work Right Cross.

Rep from * for patt.

MORE INVOLVED PATTERNS

The examples so far have shown what a simple rope cable can look like when one of the strands is changed. But what about making both the stitches and the cables more complex? Let's start with an easy one. A sand or shadow cable is just a left rope and right rope in a half-drop formation. In stockinette, it looks fairly complex (but you now know how easy it really is).

Changing half the strands to garter stitch adds even more intrigue. The garter stitch of one cable will sometimes touch the garter of the cable next door, and the stockinette does the same. It looks complicated, but when you break it up into its components, you can see how simple it is. Chart the back to know what you'll get ahead of time even before working the swatch.

In the Staghorn Cabled Coat on page 78, I took the Vs of the basic staghorn cable from page 48 and threw in some garter strands. On the first crossing row, a right cross and left cross with garter on top create a garter staghorn; next door, a right cross and left cross with ribbing on top create a ribbed staghorn. After the next cable row, the order changes. Furthermore, the back of a garter staghorn is a ribbed staghorn, and the back of a ribbed staghorn is a garter staghorn.

The classic "OXO" or Hugs and Kisses cable pattern is also used in textured reversible projects. On page 71, the O's are in garter stitch and the X's are in ribbing. On the back, although there's an O behind the X and an X behind the O, the textures are the same—the O's are still in garter and the X's are still in ribbing.

Sand Cable in Garter and Rib

CO 40 sts (4 sts per set × 10 sets).

ROW 1: *[K1, p1] 2 times, k4; rep from * to end.

ROW 2: *K4, [k1, p1] 2 times; rep from * to end.

ROW 3: (first crossing row; 4/4LC) *[K1, p1] 2 times, k4, sl 4 sts to cn and hold in front, k4 from left needle, [k1, p1] 2 times from cn; rep from * 1 time, [k1, p1] 2 times, k4.

ROWS 4 AND 6: K4, *[k1, p1] 4 times, k8; rep from * to last 4 sts, [k1, p1] 2 times.

ROW 5: [K1, p1] 2 times, *k8, [k1, p1] 4 times; rep from * to last 4 sts, k4.

ROW 7: (second crossing row; 4/4RC) *Sl 4 sts to cn and hold in back, k4 from left needle, [k1, p1] 2 times from cn, k4, [k1, p1] 2 times; rep from * 1 time, sl 4 sts to cn and hold in back, k4 from left needle, [k1, p1] 2 times from cn.

ROWS 8 AND 10: *[K1, p1] 2 times, k4; rep from * to end.

ROW 9: *K4, [k1, p1] 2 times; rep from * to end.

ROW 11: (third crossing row; 4/4LC) *K4, [k1, p1] 2 times, sl 4 sts to cn and hold in front, [k1, p1] 2 times from left needle, k4 from cn; rep from * 1 time, k4, [k1, p1] 2 times.

ROWS 12 AND 14: [K1, p1] 2 times, *k8, [k1, p1] 4 times; rep from * 1 time, k4.

ROW 13: K4, *[k1, p1] 4 times, k8; rep from * 1 time, [k1, p1] 2 times.

ROW 15: (fourth crossing row; 4/4RC) *Sl 4 sts to cn and hold in back, [k1, p1] 2 times from left needle, k4 from cn, [k1, p1] 2 times, k4; rep from * 1 time, sl 4 sts to cn and hold in back, [k1, p1] 2 times from left needle, k4 from cn.

ROWS 16: *K4, [k1, p1] 2 times; rep from * to end.

Rep Rows 1–16 for patt.

FRONT

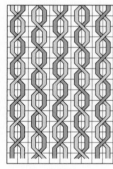

BACK

▨ ribbing
☐ garter

STITCH FILE

Textured OXO Cables

CO 48 sts (4 sts per set × 12 sets).

ROWS 1 AND 2: [K1, p1] 2 times, *k8, [k1, p1] 4 times; rep from * 1 time, k8, [k1, p1] 2 times.

ROW 3: (first crossing row) Sl 4 sts to cn and hold in front, k4 from left needle, [k1, p1] 2 times from cn, sl 4 sts to cn and hold in back, [k1, p1] 2 times from left needle, k4 from cn, sl 4 sts to cn and hold in back, k4 from left needle, [k1, p1] 2 times from cn, sl 4 sts to cn and hold in front, [k1, p1] 2 times from left needle, k4 from cn, sl 4 sts to cn and hold in front, k4 from left needle, [k1, p1] 2 times from cn, sl 4 sts to cn and hold in back, [k1, p1] 2 times from left needle, k4 from cn.

ROWS 4–10: K4, *[k1, p1] 4 times, k8; rep from * 1 time, [k1, p1] 4 times, k4.

ROW 11: (second crossing row) Sl 4 sts to cn and hold in back, [k1, p1] 2 times from left needle, k4 from cn, sl 4 sts to cn and hold in front, k4 from left needle, [k1, p1] 2 times from cn, sl 4 sts to cn and hold in front, [k1, p1] 2 times from left needle, k4 from cn, sl 4 sts to cn and hold in back, k4 from left needle, [k1, p1] 2 times from cn, sl 4 sts to cn and hold in back, [k1, p1] 2 times from left needle, k4 from cn, sl 4 sts to cn and hold in front, k4 from left needle, [k1, p1] 2 times from cn.

ROWS 12–18: [K1, p1] 2 times, *k8, [k1, p1] 4 times, rep from * 1 time, k8, [k1, p1] 2 times.

ROW 19: (third crossing row) Sl 4 sts to cn and hold in back, k4 from left needle, [k1, p1] 2 times from cn, sl 4 sts to cn and hold in front, [k1, p1] 2 times from left needle, k4 from cn, sl 4 sts to cn and hold in front, k4 from left needle, [k1, p1] 2 times from cn, sl 4 sts to cn and hold in back, [k1, p1] 2 times from left needle, k4 from cn, sl 4 sts to cn and hold in back, k4 from left needle, [k1, p1] 2 times from cn, sl 4 sts to cn and hold in front, [k1, p1] 2 times from left needle, k4 from cn.

ROWS 20–26: K4, *[k1, p1] 4 times, k8; rep from * 1 time, [k1, p1] 4 times, k4.

ROW 27: (fourth crossing row) Sl 4 sts to cn and hold in front, [k1, p1] 2 times from left needle, k4 from cn, sl

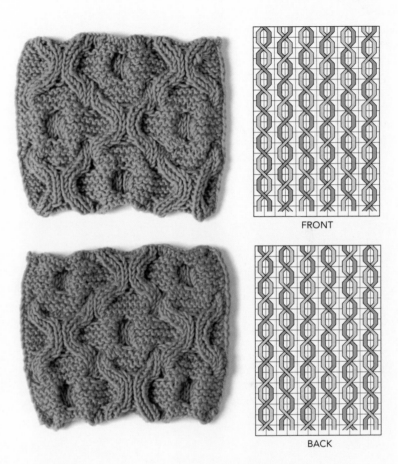

FRONT

BACK

4 sts to cn and hold in back, k4 from left needle, [k1, p1] 2 times from cn, sl 4 sts to cn and hold in back, [k1, p1] 2 times from left needle, k4 from cn, sl 4 sts to cn and hold in front, k4 from left needle, [k1, p1] 2 times from cn, sl 4 sts to cn and hold in front, [k1, p1] 2 times from left needle, k4 from cn, sl 4 sts to cn and hold in back, k4 from left needle, [k1, p1] 2 times from cn.

ROWS 28–34: [K1, p1] 2 times, *k8, [k1, p1] 4 times, rep from * 1 time, k8, [k1, p1] 2 times.

Rep Rows 3–34 for patt.

SETTING OFF STRANDS

Another way of adding more texture in a cable is to take the stitches within a strand and change the texture. The key is to keep the first and last stitches of the strand in smooth stockinette, which frames the stitches within and marks off a strand or set within a cable. This obviously means any set or strand must contain at least 3 stitches.

The swatch (Fig. 6) shows six strands of stockinette-framed texture: from right to left, seed stitch, garter stitch, slipped stitch, fagotted lace (note the uneven side edges), twisted stockinette framing stockinette, and mini-cable (1 over 1). Then cross these textures in rope cables (Fig. 7a). (I especially love the mini-cable within a cable.) As long as there is 1 stockinette stitch on each side of the texture, these will read as cables. The very organic-looking cables remind me of objects found in nature, perhaps grand old trees or tangles of seaweed. I like the sometimes phantasmagoric effect.

You might not think that these textures would read as cables on the back, but they are indeed fraternal reversible cables (Fig. 7b).

EXTRA TEXTURES

Yet another way to add texture to a cable is to utilize the long plain or interval rows between cable rows. Bands of garter or reverse stockinette can interrupt long stretches of stockinette (Fig. 8a) or rib (Fig. 8b). Garter interrupting ribbing makes the piece reversible. Embellishments such as bobbles, lace, or knit-purl textured motifs can also be placed in plain rows (Fig. 9).

Fig. 6: Stockinette-framed textured strands.

Fig. 7a: Cables in stockinette-framed textured strands.

Fig. 7b: Back of textured cables.

Fig. 8a: Reverse stockinette interrupting stockinette.

Fig. 8b: Garter interrupting ribbing.

Fig. 9: Bobbles, lace, and knit-purl combinations within stockinette of cable.

STITCH FILE

Dropped-stitch Cable

Using the long-tail method (see Glossary), CO 9 sts.

ROW 1: (RS; set-up row) K2, k1 through the back loop (tbl), k1 (dropped st), k6 (cable), k1 (dropped st), k1 tbl, k2.

ROW 2 AND ALL WS ROWS: P2, p1 tbl, p1, p6, p1, p1 tbl, p2.

ROW 3: (cable crossing row) K2, k1 tbl, k1, sl 3 sts to cn and hold in front, k3, k3 from cn, k1, k1 tbl, k2.

ROWS 5 AND 7: Rep Row 1.

ROW 9: (cable crossing row) K2, k1 tbl, k1, sl 3 sts to cn and hold in back, k3, k3 from cn, k1, k1 tbl, k2.

ROW 11: Rep Row 1.

ROW 13: K3, drop next st, use the backward-loop or cable method to CO 3 sts, k6, drop next st, CO 3 sts, k3.

Bind off on next row all 18 stitches. Ladder down both the dropped sts and there you have it.

DROPPED STITCHES

If you drop a stitch from the needle and let it run like pantyhose, "ladders" form. This is a down-and-dirty way of creating a lacy fabric. Combined with cables, dropped stitches can lighten up a piece considerably. Cabled fabrics tend to be dense and scrunched up, but the airiness of dropped stitches combats this density. If a cabled piece has dropped stitches between cables instead of reverse stockinette stitch, the piece has cobwebby openness between the cables.

Dropped stitch ladders have another advantage: For every dropped stitch, you gain twice the width of that stitch. For instance, if the gauge is 4 stitches per inch, 1 stitch measures one-quarter inch across. If this stitch drops and is allowed to ravel all the way down, the space created is three-quarters of an inch across, or a gain of a half-inch.

If you look at the loop construction of a stitch on the needle, it looks almost like a circle. There is a mathematical law that if you know the widest point of a circle (also known as the diameter), then you know how far it is around the outside of the circle (or the circumference). Multiply the width by pi (about 3.14) to arrive at the circumference. Thus, the length of yarn that makes up a stitch is about 3 times the width of the stitch.

Alas, these dropped-stitch fabrics tend to be unstable. Actually, the stitch on either side of the drop is the unstable part; with a long, loose strand next to it, the stitch distorts and enlarges. Cables help to alleviate this a bit. Another way to deal with this is to work a twisted stitch on either side of the drop—that is, work into the back loops of the stitch before and after the stitch to be dropped. Work the dropped stitch in

stockinette to let it run more easily.

Note the gap where the stitches are dropped and the fact that three stitches are cast on over it. The long-tail cast-on is suited to a dropped-stitch pattern because a knitted or cable cast-on will allow the rest of the cast-on stitches to ravel.

Dropped-stitch patterns can also be made reversible by adding ribbles. The area between strands of a cable can even vary, as for traveling-stitch cables. To create a space between or to separate two strands of a cable, work a yarnover between them. To close the space between two strands in order for them to cross, drop the stitch formed by the yarnover, allowing the strands to touch one another by spanning the gap. The dropped stitch does not run below the yarnover. The yarnover acts like a stopper, since it marks the creation of a new stitch.

TEXTURED
tote bag

FINISHED SIZE

5" (12.5 cm) bottom and side, 16½" (42 cm) wide, 11" (28 cm) tall, 24" (61 cm) straps.

YARN

Worsted weight (Medium #4).
Shown here: Berroco Linen Jeans (70% rayon, 30% linen; 80 yd [73 m]/50 g): Fiddlehead #7443, 12 skeins.

NEEDLES

U.S. size 5 (3.75 mm): 24" (60 cm) circular (cir) and set of 4 double-pointed (dpn). Adjust needle size if necessary to obtain the correct gauge.

NOTIONS

Stitch markers (m); 4 stitch holders; cable needle (cn); tapestry needle.

GAUGE

31 sts and 36 rnds = 4" (10 cm) in Body patt. 36 sts = 5" (12.5 cm) in Bottom patt (without selvedges).

This roomy tote will expand to accommodate lots of stuff. The gnarly textures are accentuated by the use of the tape yarn. If you desire a lining, I suggest ironing on a backing of nonwoven fusible interfacing fabric. This stabilizes the piece and no sewing is required. This natural yarn can withstand the heat of a pressing iron.

NOTE

Bottom of tote is worked first, then sts are picked up from all sides and worked upward in the round.

stitch guide

3/3RC (3 over 3 left cross): Sl 3 sts to cn and hold in front of work, k3, k3 from cn.

3/3RC (3 over 3 right cross): Sl 3 sts to cn and hold in back of work, k3, k3 from cn.

Bottom Pattern

(38 STS, OR 36 STS + 2)

ROW 1: (WS) K1 (selvedge st), [p3, k3] twice, p3, k6, [p3, k3] twice, p3, k1 (selvedge st).

ROW 2: K1 (selvedge st), k3, 3/3LC, 3/3RC, k6, 3/3LC, 3/3RC, k3, k1 (selvedge st).

ROWS 3, 5, AND 7: K1 (selvedge st), [k3, p3] twice, k3, p6, [k3, p3] twice, k3, k1 (selvedge st).

ROWS 4 AND 6: Knit.

ROW 8: K1 (selvedge st), k3, 3/3RC, 3/3LC, k6, 3/3RC, 3/3LC, k3, k1 (selvedge st).

ROWS 9 AND 11: Rep Row 1.

ROWS 10 AND 12: Knit.

Rep Rows 1–12 for patt.

Body Pattern

(MULTIPLE OF 33 STS)

RND 1: *K3, [p3, k3] twice, p6, [k3, p3] twice; rep from * to end.

RND 2: *K3, 3/3LC, 3/3RC, k6, 3/3LC, 3/3RC; rep from * to end.

RNDS 3, 5 AND 7: *P3, [k3, p3] twice, k6, [p3, k3] twice; rep from * to end.

RNDS 4 AND 6: Knit.

RND 8: *K3, 3/3RC, 3/3LC, k6, 3/3RC, 3/3LC; rep from * to end.

RNDS 9 AND 11: Rep Rnd 1.

RNDS 10 AND 12: Knit.

Rep Rnds 1–12 for patt.

TOTE

Bottom

With cir needle and cable or crochet method (see Glossary), CO 38 sts.

Set-up row: (RS) Knit.

Rep Rows 1–12 of Bottom pattern from chart or stitch guide 10 times, then rep Rows 1–9 once more.

Next row: K2tog, knit to last 2 sts, ssk—36 sts rem. Do not turn.

Body

With RS facing, rotate Bottom piece 90° and place marker (pm). Pick up and knit (see Glossary) 129 sts along side of Bottom, pm, pick up and knit 36 sts along CO edge, pm, pick up and knit 129 sts along other long edge, pm (leaving 36 sts from bottom unworked)—330 sts. Join for working in the rnd.

Work in Body patt until piece measures 10" (25.5 cm) high from pick-up row, ending after Rnd 2 of patt.

Border

Next rnd: [k1, p1] 8 times, k1, p2tog, *[k1, p1] 15 times, k1, p2tog; rep from * to last 14 sts, [k1, p1] 7 times—320 sts rem. Work [k1, p1] rib as established for 1" (2.5 cm).

Next rnd: (strap set-up rnd) BO 55 sts in rib patt, *[k1, p1] 9 times, k2* (21 sts on right needle for shoulder strap), BO 43 sts in rib patt, rep from * to *, BO 75 sts in patt, rep from * to *, BO 43 sts in rib patt, rep from * to *, BO rem 20 sts of rnd. Cut yarn and draw through last st of rnd.

Textured Cables

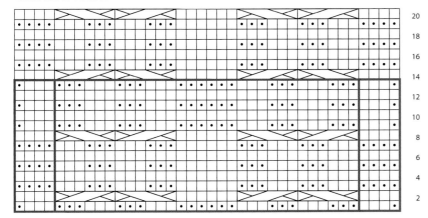

		k on RS; p on WS
	•	p on RS; k on WS
	⧓	sl 3 sts onto cn, hold in back, k3, k3 from cn
	⧓	sl 3 sts onto cn, hold in front, k3, k3 from cn
▢		body
▢		bottom

Straps

*With RS facing, join yarn to beg of held sts for one strap.

Next row: (RS) K1, [k1, p1] 9 times, k2.

Next row and all WS rows: Sl 1 st purlwise (pwise) with yarn in front (wyf), [p1, k1] 9 times, p1, sl 1 st pwise wyf.

Next row and all RS rows: K1, [k1, p1] 9 times, k2.

Rep last 2 rows until strap measures 12" (30.5 cm), ending after a WS row. Place rem sts on a holder.

Rep from * for rem 3 straps.

Finishing

Replace held sts of one strap on 1 dpn. Replace held sts of strap from same side of bag on another dpn. Join sts by grafting or 3-needle BO (see Glossary). Rep for rem 2 straps. Weave in ends.

FINISHED MEASUREMENTS

45" (114.5 cm) bust circumference, measured closed, and 26½" (67.5 cm) long.

YARN

Worsted (Medium #4).
Shown here: Mondial Dolce Mohair (60% kid mohair, 40% acrylic; 165 yd [151 m]/50 g): Mustard #136, 9 skeins.

NEEDLES

U.S. size 7 (4.5 mm). Adjust needle size if necessary to obtain the correct gauge

NOTIONS

Cable needle (cn); stitch markers (m); stitch holders; tapestry needle.

GAUGE

16 sts and 20 rows = 4" (10 cm) in St st, steam blocked and hung.
32-st staghorn cable = 4½" (11.5 cm).

STAGHORN
cabled coat

Reversible cables create a variety of possible looks in this sweater. The sleeves convert from three-quarter to full length by turning down the cuffs. You can fold back the lapels in warmer weather or close them against a cool breeze. With fully reversible lapels and cuffs, the options for wearing this coat are plenty. Wear it belted, closed with a shawl pin, or open.

stitch guide

4/4RC RG (Right cross 4 rib sts over 4 garter sts):
Sl next 4 sts to cn and hold in back, [k1, p1] twice from left needle, k4 from cn.

4/4LC RG (Left cross 4 rib sts over 4 garter sts):
Sl next 4 sts to cn and hold in front, k4 from left needle, [k1, p1] twice from cn.

4/4RC GR (Right cross 4 garter sts over 4 rib sts):
Sl next 4 sts to cn and hold in back, k4 from left needle, [k1, p1] twice from cn.

4/4LC GR (Left cross 4 garter sts over 4 rib sts):
Sl next 4 sts to cn and hold in front, [k1, p1] twice from left needle, k4 from cn.

Staghorn Pattern

(MULTIPLE OF 32 STS)

ROW 1: (RS) *K4 (garter st), [k1, p1] 4 times (rib), k4 (garter st), [k1, p1] 2 times (rib), k8 (garter st), [k1, p1] 2 times (rib); rep from * to end.

ROW 2: *[K1, p1] 2 times (rib), k8 (garter st), [k1, p1] 2 times (rib), k4 (garter st), [k1, p1] 4 times (rib), k4 (garter st); rep from * to end.

ROW 3: *4/4RC RG, 4/4LC RG, 4/4RC GR, 4/4LC GR; rep from * to end.

ROW 4: *K4, [k1, p1] 4 times, k4, [k1, p1] 2 times, k8, [k1, p1] 2 times; rep from * to end.

ROW 5: *[K1, p1] 2 times, k8, [k1, p1] 2 times, k4, [k1, p1] 4 times; rep from * to end.

ROWS 6–10: Rep Rows 4 and 5.

ROW 11: 4/4RC GR, 4/4LC GR, 4/4RC RG, 4/4LC RG; rep from * to end.

ROW 12: Rep Row 2.

ROWS 13–16: Rep Rows 1 and 2.

Rep Rows 1–16 for patt.

BACK

CO 162 sts.

Keeping first and last sts of each row in St st (selvedge), work Staghorn patt from chart or Stitch Guide. Work Rows 1–16, then rep Rows 1–4 (20 rows total), ending after a WS row; piece measures about 3½" (9 cm).

Next row: (dec row) K1, *[k1, k2tog 4 times] 8 times, k1*, [k2tog, k1] 2 times, k2tog 2 times, [k1, k2tog] 2 times; rep from * to * once—92 sts rem.

Work in St st until piece measures 16½" (42 cm), ending after a WS row.

Shape Armholes

BO 6 sts at beg of next 2 rows—80 sts rem.

Next row: (RS; dec row) K2, k2tog, work to last 4 sts, ssk, k2—2 sts dec'd.

Next row: Work even in St st.

Rep last 2 rows 6 more times—66 sts rem after last dec.

Work even in St st until armhole measures 8½" (21.5 cm), ending after a RS row.

Shape Back Neck

Next row: (WS) P19, join a new ball of yarn and BO 28 sts, purl to end.

LEFT SHOULDER

Next row: (RS) Knit to last 4 sts, ssk, k2—1 st dec. Work 1 WS row even.

Next row: Bind off 4 sts, knit to last 4 sts, ssk, k2—5 sts dec. Work 1 WS row even.

Next row: Bind off 4 sts, knit to end. Work 1 WS row even. Rep last 2 rows once. BO rem 5 sts.

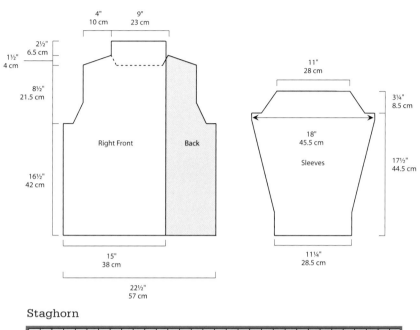

4"
10 cm

9"
23 cm

2½"
6.5 cm

1½"
4 cm

8½"
21.5 cm

Right Front

Back

16½"
42 cm

15"
38 cm

22½"
57 cm

11"
28 cm

3¼"
8.5 cm

18"
45.5 cm

Sleeves

17½"
44.5 cm

11¼"
28.5 cm

Staghorn

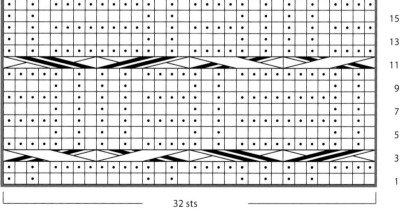

15
13
11
9
7
5
3
1

32 sts

☐ k on RS; p on WS

• p on RS; k on WS

▨ 4/4RC RG (see Stitch Guide)

▨ 4/4LC RG (see Stitch Guide)

▨ 4/4RC GR (see Stitch Guide)

▨ 4/4LC GR (see Stitch Guide)

☐ pattern repeat box

RIGHT SHOULDER
Next row: (RS) K2, k2tog, knit to end—
  1 st dec'd.
Work 1 WS row even. Rep decrease
row once.
Next row: (WS) Bind off 4 sts, purl
  to end.
Work 1 RS row even. Rep last 2 rows
twice. BO rem 5 sts.

LEFT FRONT

CO 98 sts.
  Keeping first and last sts of each row
in St st (selvedge), work Staghorn patt.
Work Rows 1–16, then rep Rows 1–4 (20
rows total), ending after a WS row; piece
measures about 3½" (9 cm).
Next row: (RS; dec row) K1, *k1, k2tog,
  [K1, k2tog twice] 3 times; rep from *
  once, k1, k2tog, [k1, k2tog twice] 2 times
  (30 sts), place marker (pm), work Staghorn patt to last st, k1—79 sts rem.
Work St st and Staghorn patt as established until piece measures 16½" (42 cm),
ending after a WS row.

Shape Armholes
Work armhole shaping at beg of RS rows
as for back—66 sts rem. Work even until
armhole measures 8½" (21.5 cm), ending
after a WS row.

Shape Shoulder
*Next row: (RS) BO 4 sts, work to
  end—62 sts. Work 1 WS row even.
Rep from * 2 more times—54 sts rem.
Next row: (RS) BO 5 sts, work to
  end—49 sts rem.
Work one more row of Staghorn patt. Sl
rem 49 sts to stitch holder and cut yarn.

RIGHT FRONT

Work as for Left Front until piece measures 3½" (9 cm), ending before dec row.

Next row: (RS; dec row) K1, work Staghorn patt over next 48 sts, pm, *[k2tog twice, K1] 3 times, k2tog, k1; rep from *, [k2tog twice, k1] 2 times, k2tog, k1—79 sts rem.

Work St st and Staghorn patt as established until piece measures 16½" (42 cm), ending after a RS row.

Shape Armholes
Work armhole shaping at beg of WS rows as for back—66 sts rem. Work even until armhole measures 8½" (21.5 cm), ending after a RS row.

Shape Shoulder
*Next row: (WS) Bind off 4 sts, work to end—62 sts. Work 1 RS row even. Rep from * 2 more times—54 sts rem.

Next row: (WS) Bind off 5 sts, work to end—49 sts rem. Sl rem sts to stitch holder; do not cut yarn.

SLEEVES

CO 82 sts.

Keeping first and last sts of each row in St st (selvedge), work Staghorn patt 2 times, work first 16 sts of Staghorn patt once more. Work Rows 2–16 of patt, then rep Rows 1–4 (20 rows total), ending after a WS row; piece measures about 3½" (9 cm).

Next row: (RS; dec row) K1 (selvedge), [k1, k2tog 3 times] 5 times, [k1, k2tog]

twice, [k2tog, k1] twice, [k2tog 3 times, k1] 5 times—48 sts rem.

Work even in St st for 3 rows.

Next row: (RS; inc row) K2, M1, knit to last 2 sts, M1, k2—2 sts inc'd; 50 sts.

Rep inc row every 4th row 7 times, then every 6th row 5 times—74 sts.

Work even in St st until piece measures 18" (45.5 cm), ending after a WS row.

SHAPE CAP

BO 6 sts at beg of next 2 rows—62 sts rem.

Next row: (RS; dec row) K2, k2tog, work to last 4 sts, ssk, k2—2 sts dec'd.

Next row: Work even in St st.

Rep last 2 rows 6 more times—48 sts rem after last dec. BO rem sts on RS.

FINISHING

Block piece to measurements. Sew shoulder seams. Set in sleeve, easing fabric as needed. Sew side and sleeve seams.

Collar
With RS facing, work across 49 sts of Right Front, pick up and knit (see Glossary) 64 sts evenly across Back Neck as foll: k1 in each row along right back edge, k1 in first st of back neck, *k1 in next st, [k1 in space between last st and next st, k1 in next st] 4 times; rep from * 4 times, k1 in each of next 2 sts, k1 in each row along left back edge, cont 49 Staghorn patt sts of Left Front—162 sts.

Work Staghorn patt over all sts until piece measures 2½" (6.5 cm). BO tightly in patt. Weave in loose ends.

traveling stitch
cables

There are times when thin vertical columns of knits floating
on a sea of purls want to cross over one another, but they may
be far apart. In order for these small knit wales to come
together to cross, they must travel across a vast expanse of
purls. Such are traveling stitches—knit stitches cross over
purls in little baby steps until they are next to each other.
Even when not crossing with other knits, these are still
cables because of the unseen crossings of knits with purls.
(Because of the large repeats and multiples involved in many
traveling stitch patterns, the Stitch Files in this chapter are
shown only in charts.

CROSSINGS, SEEN AND UNSEEN

There can be many single knit lines traveling at once in different directions. They can get together with other lone knit lines and cross any time they get together. It can be an intricate dance. Bavarian twisted stitches (see next page) follow this principle, but the knit stitches are worked through their back loops.

Sometimes the knits don't cross with any other knits at all; they seem to roam alone. In fact they do cross, but only with purls, in order to travel across the fabric. In the Background Stitches Cable Vest on page 92, the traveling stitches are close together and look almost like a roaming pack of knits. In the swatch at right, the roaming knit stitches are farther apart, with more room to breathe.

STITCH FILE

Single Traveling Stitch Cable

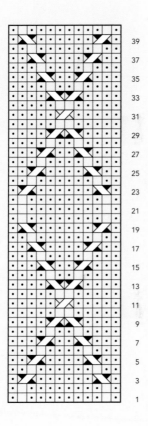

☐ k on RS; p on WS

· p on RS; k on WS

sl 1 st to cn and hold in back, k1 from left needle, k1 from cn

sl 1 st to cn and hold in front, k1 from left needle, k1 from cn

Multiple Single Traveling Stitches

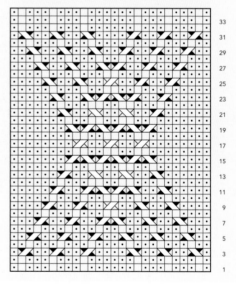

□ k on RS; p on WS

⊡ p on RS; k on WS

⊠ sl 1 st to cn and hold in back, k1 from left needle, p1 from cn

⊠ sl 1 st to cn and hold in front, p1 from left needle, k1 from cn

⊠ sl 1 st to cn and hold in back, k1 from left needle, k1 from cn

⊠ sl 1 st to cn and hold in front, k1 from left needle, k1 from cn

⊠ k1 tbl on RS; p1 tbl on WS

Bavarian Twisted Stitches

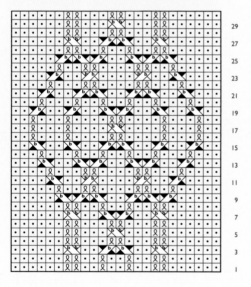

 sl 1 st to cn and hold in back, k1 tbl from left needle, k1 tbl from cn

sl 1 st to cn and hold in front, k1 tbl from left needle, k1 tbl from cn

sl 1 st to cn and hold in back, k1 tbl from left needle, p1 from cn

sl 1 st to cn and hold in front, p1 from left needle, k1 tbl from cn

sl 3 sts to cn and hold in back, k3 from left needle, p3 from cn

sl 3 sts to cn and hold in front, p3 from left needle, k3 from cn

STITCH FILE

Non-crossing Single Traveling Stitches

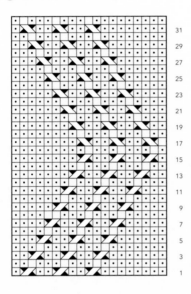

STITCH FILE

Wider Traveling Cables

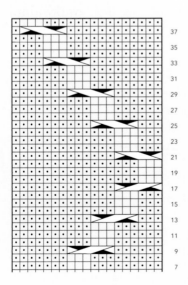

Fig. 2: These traveling stitches cross in complex patterns.

Traveling knit stitches sometimes buddy up and travel with a companion. The result is not thin lines of lone knit stitches but a group or cluster of knit stitches traveling across a piece, as in the Five-way Cabled Shrug on page 100 (Fig. 2). These wider knit wales (six of them) not only cross with one another, they can cross and form a cable all by themselves. It's as if the roaming pack has relationships among themselves as well as with other groups.

These larger bunches of knits can not only travel across 1 purl stitch one at a time, such as the 1-stitch traveling stitches, they can take larger steps by crossing over 2, 3, or even more purl stitches. They get to their destination faster this way.

CHARTING

Traveling stitches can still be charted using my charting system. Consider the basic rope cable. See how it can expand by a few boxes **(Fig. 3)**. Although still a rope, it has opened up with more breathing space. Use this concept to expand other cables such as braids **(Fig. 4)** and basketweaves **(Fig. 5)**.

Use my charting method to see the "bigger picture" of how you want the cables to look. You may have to chart them the old fashioned way, stitch by stitch and row by row, to fill in the details of exactly how many stitches the strands move.

BACKGROUND STITCHES

Different background or filler stitches can frame these traveling cables. In the expanded traveling ropes at right, the stitches between the strands in the rope can be filled with seed or moss or even garter stitch instead of reverse stockinette **(Fig. 6)**. You can even change things up with moss or seed or garter as the background and reverse stockinette for the centers **(Fig. 7)**. Instead of setting cables against other textures such as reverse stockinette or seed or moss, keep everything in stockinette for a very subtle bas relief effect **(Fig. 8)**.

Leaving lots of "empty" background allows you to suddenly introduce a cable. Where there was nothing but reverse stockinette stitch before, change a few stitches to stockinette, then set them off to travel and cable. A cable seems to pop up out of nowhere and emerge, only to disappear again **(Fig. 9)**.

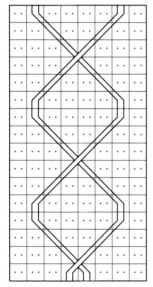

Fig. 3: Chart of traveling rope.

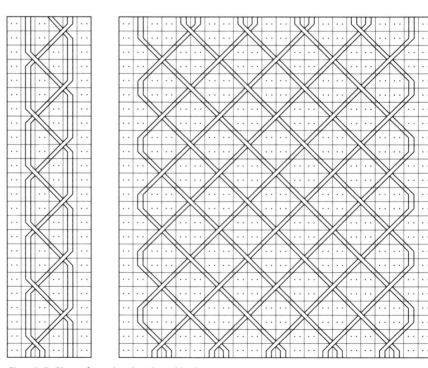

Figs. 4–5: Chart of traveling braids and basketweaves.

Fig. 6: Traveling diamond filled with moss stitch.

Fig. 7: Traveling diamond filled with reverse stockinette stitch on garter background.

Fig. 8: Traveling ropes in stockinette.

Fig. 9: Cable emerging out of nowhere.

Diamond and Diagonal Cables

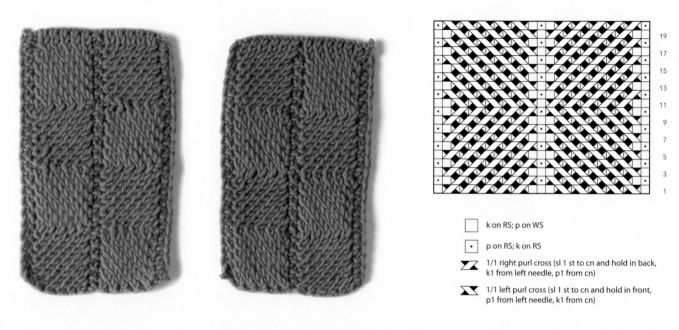

☐ k on RS; p on WS

▪ p on RS; k on RS

◣◥ 1/1 right purl cross (sl 1 st to cn and hold in back, k1 from left needle, p1 from cn)

◤◢ 1/1 left purl cross (sl 1 st to cn and hold in front, p1 from left needle, k1 from cn)

REVERSIBILITY

Lone traveling stitches, whether a single line of knits or even a larger group of ribs, do not translate well to reversibility. If I were to chart these as ribbles (ribbed reversible cables), the back would just look like a few errant cable crosses. While not exactly random, it does not read strongly as a pattern **(Fig. 10)**.

Instead, work lines of knits and purls (1x1 rib) all traveling in the same direction. Unlike the stitches from the Background Stitches Cable Vest, view these same stitches as knits over purls rather than knits over knits for the diamonds. The

diagonals are already reversible because they are worked over ribbing. The traveling diagonal stitches on the side patterns of the vest are already reversible; follow the pattern for either to see how they work.

Don't confine yourself to one knit crossed with one purl or vice versa. Try two knits and two purls for a more plumped-up version, or even three knits and three purls for even more drama.

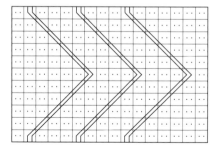
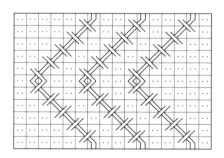

Fig. 10: My charts of fronts and backs of reversible cables.

STITCH FILE

Traveling Diamonds

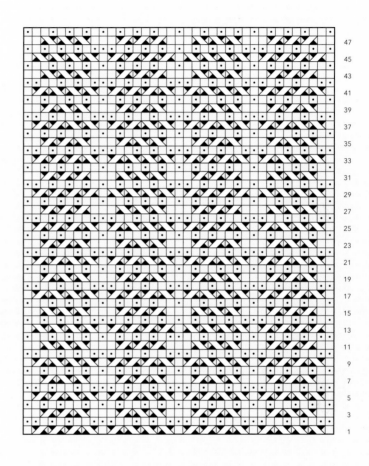

| | k on RS; p on WS |
| · | p on RS; k on RS |

1/1 right purl cross (sl 1 st to cn and hold in back, k1 from left needle, p1 from cn)

1/1 left purl cross (sl 1 st to cn and hold in front, p1 from left needle, k1 from cn)

BACKGROUND STITCHES
cable vest

Cables aren't always worked over many stitches. The traveling stitches of this vest are just one stitch crossed over another. Worked in alpaca, the piece is especially warm because of the dimensions of the stitch patterns. The sides and front panel show two different varieties of traveling stitch pattern. This classic sweater suits both guys and girls.

FINISHED SIZES
37½ (39, 42½, 45½, 49)" (95 [99, 108, 115.5, 124.5] cm) chest circumference and 22¼ (22¼, 22¼, 24, 24)" (56.5 [56.5, 56.5, 61, 61] cm) from bottom of ribbing to shoulder; designed for a loose fit. Vest shown measures 39" (95 cm).

YARN
DK weight (Light #3).
Shown here: Louet Eastport (70% alpaca, 30% merino wool; 150 yd [137 m]/75 g): Snowy Natural #06, 6 (6, 7, 8, 8) skeins.

NEEDLES
U.S. size 7 (4.5 mm): straight or circular (cir).
U.S. size 5 (3.75 mm): 16" (40 cm) cir. Adjust needle sizes if necessary to obtain the correct gauge.

NOTIONS
Stitch markers (m); cable needle (cn); tapestry needle.

GAUGE
18-st rep of cabled center panel = 2¾" (7 cm).
24-st rep of side panel patt = 3¼" (8.5 cm).
31 rows = 4" (10 cm) in all patterns.

NOTES

Markers indicate side patterns and center panel. Slip markers (sl m) as you come to them.
V-neck decreases are specifically designed to coordinate with the stitch pattern, so the row count is also specific. To keep the pattern properly lined up with neck decreases, body length can be adjusted in 16-row increments only and by changing starting point for first row above rib. Be aware of total lengths and adjust accordingly.
Stitch count around V-neck can be adjusted in multiples of 4 stitches, as desired. Make sure to pick up the same number of stitches along both sides of the front neck.

stitch guide

RC (1 over 1 Right Cross): Sl 1 st to cn and hold in back, k1 from left needle, k1 from cn.

LC (1 over 1 Left Cross): Sl 1 st to cn and hold in front, k1 from left needle, k1 from cn.

RT (1K over 1P Right Cross): Sl 1 purl st to cn and hold in back, k1 from left needle, p1 from cn.

LT (1K over 1P Left Cross): Sl 1 knit st to cn and hold in front, p1 from left needle, k1 from cn.

Right-Side Panel

(MULTIPLE OF 24 STS + 3)

ROW 1: (RS) K2, p1, work 6 (12, 18, 0, 6) st(s) at beg of chart according to your size, *[k1, p1] 6 times, k1, RT 5 times, p1; rep from * 0 (0, 0, 1, 1) time.

ROW 2: * K1, p1, RT 5 times, (k1, p1) 6 times; rep from * 0 (0, 0, 1, 1) time, work next 6 (12, 18, 0, 6) sts of chart according to your size, k1, p2.

ROWS 3, 5, 7, AND 9: Rep Row 1.

ROWS 4, 6, 8, AND 10: Rep Row 2.

ROW 11: K2, p1, work 6 (12, 18, 0, 6) st(s) at beg of chart according to your size, *k1, RT 5 times, [p1, k1] 6 times, p1; rep from * 0 (0, 0, 1, 1) time.

ROW 12: * [K1, p1] 7 times, RT 5 times; rep from * 0 (0, 0, 1, 1) time, work next 6 (12, 18, 0, 6) st(s) of chart according to your size, p1.

ROWS 13, 15, 17, AND 19: Rep Row 11.

ROWS 14, 16, 18, AND 20: Rep Row 12.

Rep Rows 1–20 for patt.

Left-Side Panel

(MULTIPLE OF 24 STS + 3)

ROW 1: (RS) *P1, LT 5 times, [k1, p1] 6 times, k1; rep from * 0 (0, 0, 1, 1) time, work next 6 (12, 18, 0, 6) st(s) of chart according to your size, p1, k2.

ROW 2: P2, k1, work next 6 (12, 18, 0, 6) st(s) of chart according to your size, *[p1, k1] 6 times, LT 5 times; rep from * 0 (0, 0, 1, 1) time, p1, k1.

ROWS 3, 5, 7, AND 9: Rep Row 1.

ROWS 4, 6, 8, AND 10: Rep Row 2.

ROW 11: *(P1, k1) 6 times, p1, LT 5 times, k1; rep from * 0 (0, 0, 1, 1) time, work next 6 (12, 18, 0, 6) st(s) of chart according to your size, p1, k2.

ROW 12: P2, k1, work next 6 (12, 18, 0, 6) st(s) of chart according to your size, *LT 5 times, [p1, k1] 7 times; rep from * 0 (0, 0, 1, 1) time.

ROWS 13, 15, 17, AND 19: Rep Row 11.

ROWS 14, 16, 18, AND 20: Rep Row 12.

Rep Rows 1–20 for patt.

Center Panel

(WORKED OVER 57 STS)

ROW 1: (RS) K1, p1, *LC 3 times, RC, k1, LC, RC 3 times, k1; rep from * 2 more times, end last rep RC 3 times, p1, k1.

ROW 2 AND ALL EVEN OR WS ROWS: P1, k1, p53, k1, p1.

ROW 3: K1, p1, *k1, LC 2 times, RC, k3, LC, RC 2 times, k2; rep from * 2 more times, end last rep with k1 only instead of k2, p1, k1.

ROW 5: K1, p1, *LC 2 times, RC 2 times, k1; rep from * 5 more times, end last rep RC 2 times, p1, k1.

ROW 7: K1, p1, *k1, LC, RC 2 times, k3, LC 2 times, RC, k2; rep from * 2 more times, end last rep with k1 only instead of k2, p1, k1.

ROW 9: K1, p1, *LC, RC 3 times, k1, LC 3 times, RC, k1; rep from * 2 more times, end last rep RC, p1, k1.

ROW 11: K1, p1, *k1, RC 3 times, k3, LC 3 times, k2; rep from * 2 more times, end last rep with k1 only instead of k2, p1, k1.

ROW 13: K1, p1, *RC 4 times, k1, LC 4 times, k1; rep from * 2 more times, end last rep LC 4 times, p1, k1.

ROW 15: Rep Row 11.

ROW 17: Rep Row 9.

ROW 19: Rep Row 7.

ROW 21: Rep Row 5.

ROW 23: Rep Row 3.

ROW 25: Rep Row 1.

ROW 27: K1, p1, * k1, LC 3 times, k3, RC 3 times, k2; rep from * 2 more times, end last rep with k1 only instead of k2, p1, k1.

ROW 29: K1, p1, * LC 4 times, k1, RC 4 times, k1; rep from * 2 more times, end last rep RC 4 times, p1, k1.

ROW 31: Rep Row 27.

Rep Rows 1–32 for patt.

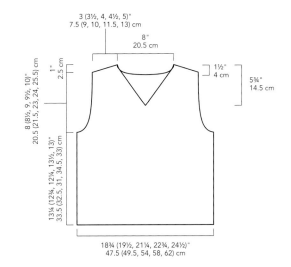

3 (3½, 4, 4½, 5)"
7.5 (9, 10, 11.5, 13) cm

8"
20.5 cm

1"
2.5 cm

1½"
4 cm

5¾"
14.5 cm

8 (8½, 9, 9½, 10)"
20.5 (21.5, 23, 24, 25.5) cm

13¾ (12¾, 12¼, 13¾, 13)"
33.5 (32.5, 31, 34.5, 33) cm

18¾ (19½, 21¼, 22¾, 24½)"
47.5 (49.5, 54, 58, 62) cm

BACK

Ribbing

With smaller needle, CO 123 (135, 147, 159, 171) sts.

Row 1 and all odd-numbered rows: (WS) P2, *k1, p1; rep from * to last st, p1.

Row 2 and all even-numbered rows: K2, *p1, k1; rep from * to last st, k1.

Rep Rows 1 and 2 until piece measures 2¾" (7 cm), ending after a WS row; on last row, place markers (pm) 33 (39, 45, 51, 57) sts from each end, with 57 sts between markers in center of row.

Body

Next row: (RS) With larger needles, work Right-Side Panel chart according to your size as foll to m: k2, p1, work next 6 (12, 18, 0, 6) st(s), work 24-st rep of Right-Side Panel 1 (1, 1, 2, 2) time(s), work Row 1 (1, 1, 15, 15) of Center Panel patt, work 24-st rep of Left-Side Panel 1 (1, 1, 2, 2) time(s), work 6 (12, 18, 0, 6) st(s), end with last 3 sts of chart. (For a vest that measures 22¼" [56.5 cm] long, beg at Row 1 of Center panel; for a vest that measures 24" [61 cm], beg at Row 15.) Continue in patt as established until piece measures 13¼ (12¾, 12¼, 13½, 13)" (33.5 [32.5, 31, 34.5, 33] cm) from CO or 9 (9½, 10, 10½, 11)" (23 [24, 25.5, 26.5, 28] cm) short of total desired length (either 22¼" or 24" [56.5 or 61 cm]), ending after a WS row.

Right-Side Panel

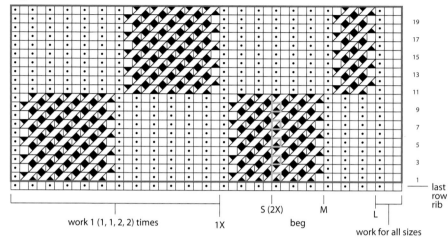

Left-Side Panel

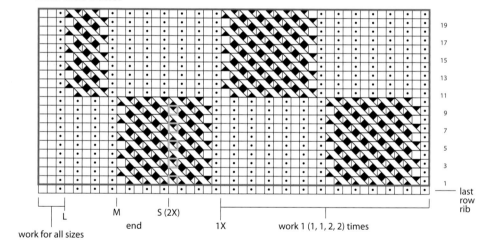

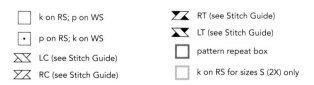

□ k on RS; p on WS

• p on RS; k on WS

⟋⟍ LC (see Stitch Guide)

⟍⟋ RC (see Stitch Guide)

◥◣ RT (see Stitch Guide)

◤◢ LT (see Stitch Guide)

□ pattern repeat box

□ k on RS for sizes S (2X) only

96

Center Panel

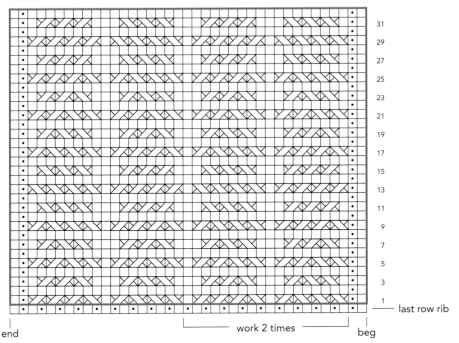

31
29
27
25
23
21
19
17
15
13
11
9
7
5
3
1 — last row rib

end | work 2 times | beg

Shape Armholes

Continuing in patt as established, BO 7 (8, 9, 10, 10) sts at beg of next 2 rows, 3 (3, 3, 3, 4) sts at beg of next 2 rows, and 2 sts at beg of next 2 rows—99 (109, 119, 129, 139) sts rem.

Next row: (RS; dec row): K2, k2tog, work in patt to last 4 sts, ssk, k2—2 sts dec'd. Continue in patt as established, rep dec row every RS row 1 (3, 5, 6, 7) more time(s)—95 (101, 107, 115, 123) sts rem.

Next row: (RS; dec row) K2, p2tog, work in patt to last 4 sts, ssp, k2—93 (99, 105, 113, 121) sts rem.

Next row: (WS) P2, k1, work in patt to last 3 sts, k1, p2.

Continue in patt as established, work even until armholes measure 7½ (8, 8½, 9, 9½)" (19 [20.5, 21.5, 23, 24] cm), ending after a RS row.

Shape Back Neck

Work 29 (32, 35, 39, 43) sts in patt as established, join a new ball of yarn and BO 35 sts, work in patt to end. Shoulders are worked separately.

Shape Right Shoulder

BO 3 sts on next WS row. Work 1 row even. BO 2 sts on next WS row.

Next row: (RS; BO row) BO 6 (6, 7, 8, 9) sts from shoulder, work to last 3 sts, k2tog, k1—17 (20, 22, 25, 28) sts rem. Work 1 row even.

Next row: (RS; BO row) BO 5 (6, 7, 8, 9), work to last 3 sts, k2tog, k1—11 (13, 14, 16, 18) sts rem. Work 1 row even.

Next row: (RS; BO row) BO 5 (6, 7, 8, 9), work to end—6 (7, 7, 8, 9) sts rem. Work 1 row even.
  BO rem sts.

Shape Left Shoulder

BO 3 sts on next RS row. Work 1 row even. BO 2 sts on next RS row.

Next row: (WS; BO row) BO 6 (6, 7, 8, 9) from shoulder, work to end—18 (21, 23, 26, 29) sts rem.

Next row: (RS; dec row) K1, ssk, work to end—1 st dec'd.

Next row: (WS; BO row) BO 5 (6, 7, 8, 9) work to end—12 (14, 15, 17, 19) sts rem.

Next row: (RS; dec row) K1, ssk, work to end—1 st dec'd.

Next row: (WS; BO row) BO 5 (6, 7, 8, 9), work to end—6 (7, 7, 8, 9) sts rem.

Work 1 row even. BO rem sts.

FRONT

Work as for Back until armholes measure 3¼ (3¾, 4¼, 4¾, 5¼)" (8 [9.5, 11, 12, 13.5] cm), ending after Row 2 of Center Panel.

Shape Front Neck

Next row: (RS) Continuing in patt as established, work 46 (49, 52, 56, 60), join a separate ball of yarn and bind off center st, work to end. Shoulders are worked separately.

Left Shoulder

Work 1 row even.

Next row: (RS; dec row) Work in patt to last 4 sts, k2tog, k2—1 st dec'd. Work 1 row even.

Rep last 2 rows 4 more times, then rep RS dec row 1 more time—40 (43, 46, 50, 54) sts rem.

Next row: (WS; dec row) P2, p2tog, work in patt to end—1 st dec'd.

Next row: (RS; dec row) Rep RS dec row—1 st dec'd.

Work 1 row even.

Rep last 2 rows 5 more times, then rep RS dec row 1 more time—32 (35, 38, 42, 46) sts rem.

Next row: (WS; dec row) P2, p2tog, work to end—1 st dec'd.

Next row: (RS; dec row) Rep RS dec row—1 st dec'd.

Work 1 row even.

Rep last 2 rows 5 more times—25 (28, 31, 35, 39) sts rem.

Next row: (RS; BO row) BO 6 (6, 7, 8, 9) sts from shoulder, work in patt to last 4 sts, k2tog, k2—18 (21, 23, 26, 29 sts rem).

Work 1 row even.

Next row: (RS; BO row) BO 5 (6, 7, 8, 9) sts, work in patt to last 4 sts, k2tog, k2—12 (14, 15, 17, 19) sts rem.

Next row: (WS; dec row) P2, p2tog, work to end—1 st dec'd.

Next row: (RS; BO row) BO 5 (6, 7, 8, 9) sts, work in patt to end—6 (7, 7, 8, 9) sts rem.

Work 1 row even. BO rem sts.

Right Shoulder

Work 1 row even.

Next row: (RS; dec row) K2, ssk, work in patt to end—1 st dec'd.

Work 1 row even.

Rep last 2 rows 4 more times, then rep RS dec row 1 more time—40 (43, 46, 50, 54) sts rem.

Next row: (WS; dec row) Work in patt to last 4 sts, ssp, p2—1 st dec'd.

Next row: (RS; dec row) Rep RS dec row—1 st dec'd.

Work 1 row even.

Rep last 2 rows 5 more times, then rep dec row once—32 (35, 38, 42, 46) sts rem.

Next row: (WS; dec row) Work in patt to last 4 sts, ssp, p2—1 st dec'd.

Next row: (RS; dec row) Rep RS dec row—1 st dec'd.

Work 1 row even.

Rep last 2 rows 4 more times, rep RS dec row 1 more time—25 (28, 31, 35, 39) sts rem.

Next row: (WS; BO row) BO 6 (6, 7, 8, 9) sts from shoulder, work in patt to end—19 (22, 24, 27, 30) sts rem.

Next row: (RS; dec row) K2, ssk, work in patt to end—1 st dec'd.

Next row: (WS; BO row) BO 5 (6, 7, 8, 9) sts, work in patt to end—13 (15, 16, 18, 20) sts rem.

Rep RS dec row 1 more time—1 st dec'd.

Next row: (WS; BO row) BO 5 (6, 7, 8, 9) sts, work in patt to last 4 sts, ssp, p2—6 (7, 7, 8, 9) sts rem.

Work 1 row even. BO rem sts.

FINISHING

Block piece to measurements. With yarn threaded on a tapestry needle, sew shoulder and side seams.

Armhole Edging

With RS facing, smaller cir needle, and beg at side seam, pick up and knit (see Glossary) 104 (112, 120, 124, 132) sts evenly spaced around armhole, pm. Join for working in the rnd. Work [k1, p1] rib for ¾" (2 cm). BO tightly in patt.

Neck Edging

With RS facing, smaller cir needle, and beg at right shoulder seam, pick up and knit 57 sts evenly along back neck, pick up and knit 34 sts evenly along left neck edge, pick up and knit 1 st over center BO and pm in this st, pick up and knit 34 sts evenly along right neck edge, pm—126 sts. Join for working in the rnd.

Rnd 1: Work [k1, p1] rib over all sts, being certain that marked center st is worked as a knit st.

Rnd 2: Work in ribbing to 1 st before marked center st, sl 2 sts tog knitwise, k1, p2sso (sl 2, k1, p2sso), continue in ribbing to end—124 sts rem.

Rnd 3: Work in ribbing to 1 st before marked center st, k1, k1 (center st), k1, work in ribbing to end.

Rep Rnds 2 and 3 two more times, then rep Rnd 2 once more—118 sts rem. BO tightly in patt.

FIVE-WAY
cabled shrug

This versatile piece will become a wardrobe staple as a shrug, wrap, poncho, or stole. With so many ways to wear it, it's good value and will stretch your wearing options—so indulge in some soft, touchable yarn and buttons you love. There are probably more than five ways to wear this accessory—how many more can you come up with?

FINISHED SIZE
16" (40.5 cm) wide and 54" (137 cm) long.

YARN
Worsted (Medium #4).
Shown here: Classic Elite Lush (50% angora, 50% wool; 123 yd [112 m]/50 g): Princess Pink #4489, 8 skeins.

NEEDLES
U.S. size 9 (5.5 mm). Adjust needle size if necessary to obtain the correct gauge.

NOTIONS
Stitch markers (m); twelve removable markers; cable needle (cn); size G/6 (4.00 mm) crochet hook; tapestry needle; twelve ½" (1.3 cm) buttons.

GAUGE
38-st cabled center panel = 5¼" (13 cm).
19 sts and 24 rows = 4" (10 cm) in scattered seed patt.

NOTE

Markers indicate scattered seed st pattern at sides of cable. Slip markers (sl m) as you come to them.

stitch guide

2/2RC (2 over 2 right cross): Sl 2 sts to cn and hold in back of work, k2, k2 from cn.

4/4LC (4 over 4 left cross): Sl 4 sts to cn and hold in front of work, k4, k4 from cn.

4/4RC (4 over 4 right cross): Sl 4 sts to cn and hold in back of work, k4, k4 from cn.

M1LP (make one left purlwise): With left needle, pick up strand between last st worked and first st on left needle from front to back and purl into back of the lifted loop—1 st inc'd.

M1RP (make one right purlwise): With left needle, pick up strand between last st worked and first st on left needle from back to front and purl into front of the lifted loop—1 st inc'd.

M2P (make two purlwise): With left needle, pick up strand between last st worked and first st on left needle from in front to back and purl into back and front of the lifted loop—2 sts inc'd.

SHRUG

CO 86 sts.

Row 1: (RS) Work Right-Side Panel chart over first 24 sts, place marker (pm), work Center Cable Panel chart over next 38 sts, pm, work Left-Side Panel chart over last 24 sts.

Continue working respective patterns until piece measures 54" (137 cm) or desired length, ending after Row 43 of Central Cable Panel chart. BO in patt.

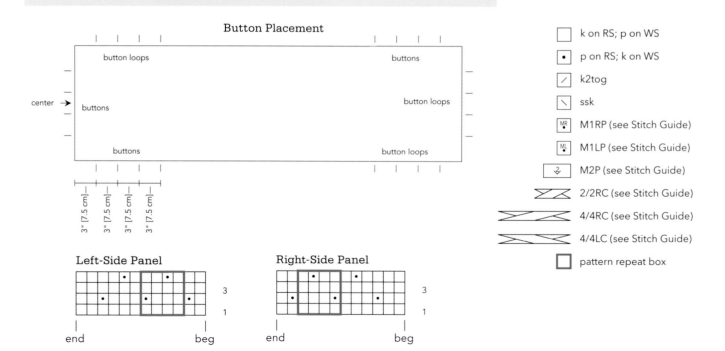

Button Placement

button loops   buttons

center →   buttons   button loops

buttons   button loops

3" [7.5 cm]   3" [7.5 cm]   3" [7.5 cm]   3" [7.5 cm]

	k on RS; p on WS
•	p on RS; k on WS
/	k2tog
\	ssk
MR•	M1RP (see Stitch Guide)
ML•	M1LP (see Stitch Guide)
⌄	M2P (see Stitch Guide)
▱▱	2/2RC (see Stitch Guide)
⬦	4/4RC (see Stitch Guide)
⬦	4/4LC (see Stitch Guide)
☐	pattern repeat box

Left-Side Panel

3
1

end   beg

Right-Side Panel

3
1

end   beg

Center Cable Panel

55
53
51
49
47
45
43
41
39
37
35
33
31
29
27
25
23
21
19
17
15
13
11
9
7
5
3
1

FINISHING

Block piece to measurements. Weave in ends.

With crochet hook and RS facing, sc evenly around all edges, working ch 2 at corners, join with slip st to first sc. (See Glossary for crochet directions.) Using removable markers, mark for 4 buttons spaced 3" (7.5 cm) apart at one short end, mark for 4 buttons spaced 3" (7.5 cm) from end and 3" (7.5 cm) apart at lower left end of long edge, mark for 4 buttons spaced 3" (7.5 cm) from end and 3" (7.5 cm) apart at upper right end of long edge (see diagram).

Next sc row: Ch 1 and turn, sc in each sc and work 3 sc in each ch-2 corner space, work buttonhole loops of (sc, ch 5, sc) all in each sc on edge opposite buttons, join with slip st to first sc.

Next sc row: Ch 1 and turn, sc in each sc and work 5 sc in each ch-5 buttonhole loop, join with slip st to first sc, fasten and end off.

Attach buttons at marked places.

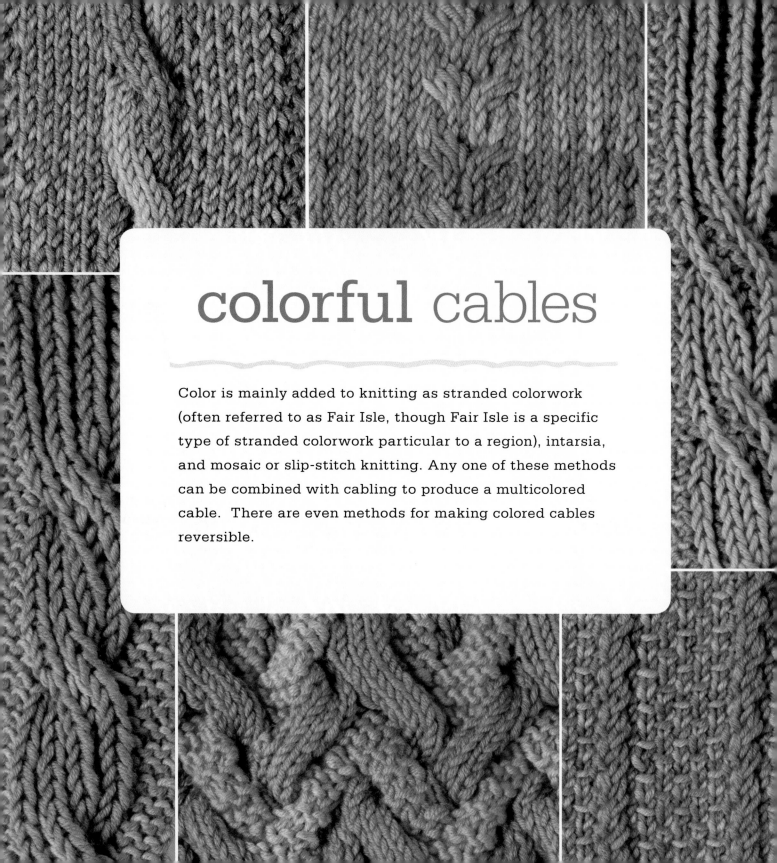

colorful cables

Color is mainly added to knitting as stranded colorwork (often referred to as Fair Isle, though Fair Isle is a specific type of stranded colorwork particular to a region), intarsia, and mosaic or slip-stitch knitting. Any one of these methods can be combined with cabling to produce a multicolored cable. There are even methods for making colored cables reversible.

ADDING COLOR TO CABLES

When it comes to adding color to cables, just because you can use the whole rainbow doesn't mean you should! A busy cable pattern over a busy color pattern will not show up successfully; the color patterns will fight with the cabled texture **(Fig. 1)**.

To prevent colored cable blindness, work the strands to be cabled in a solid color. In stranded colorwork, figure out which stitches will create the cable and work them in solid colors; the strands can be different colors for a more dramatic effect. In the Two-Colored Handbag on page 136, the strands of the cables alternate colors. I recommend keeping the rest of the stitches around the cable in a small allover color pattern such as bird's-eye at right.

Fig. 1: Cable in a busy color pattern.

STITCH FILE

Two-color Cable Surrounded by Bird's-eye Pattern

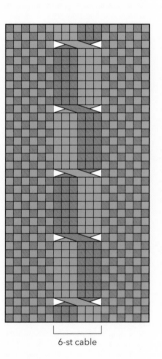

6-st cable

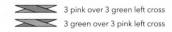
3 pink over 3 green left cross
3 green over 3 pink left cross

Fig. 2: Mosaic (slip-stitch) cables.

Fig. 3: Intarsia cables.

Fig. 4: Pinstriped cable.

Fig. 5: Mirrored pinstripe cables, with 3 stitches between.

Fig. 6: Repeating pinstripe cables.

Cables in mosaic knitting can be worked the same way as cables in stranded knitting; the sets of stitches to be cabled should be set off in a solid color (**Fig. 2**).

Intarsia is good for cables of a different color farther apart or for cables of many different colors across a piece. You don't want floats that are longer than an inch, or they may snag or distort the fabric. Rather than carry a color for too long a stretch, add a separate bobbin and work the cable stitches intarsia-style (**Fig. 3**).

Pinstripes

One exception to solid-color strands is pinstriped cables. In a pinstripe pattern, one color alternates with another color across a row, with the same colors stacked atop each other on subsequent rows. This creates vertical lines that are 1 stitch wide. Cabling a pinstripe pattern punctuates the sinuous movements of a cable, as in the Pinstriped Cable Pullover on page 112.

The minimum number of stitches in a set for the pinstripe cable pattern is 2 stitches—color A and color B (**Fig. 4**). If sets of odd-numbered stitches are crossed, the pattern will be broken up. A 3 over 3 cable, for instance, means crossing A-B-A over B-A-B. Not only is the cable not symmetrical, the pinstriped pattern is interrupted, so keep each set or strand in a pinstripe cable an even number.

Does this sound familiar? It's the same idea behind ribbles. 1x1 rib is also based on a multiple of 2. Pinstriped cables follow the same rules as ribbles. In a single pinstriped cable, the cable begins with color A and ends with color B. This is the same as for ribbles, which begin with a knit and end with a purl.

If you want a mirror-image cable, work an odd number of stitches between your cables. That way, the other cable will begin with color A and end with color B (**Fig. 5**). The A stitches of these cables

Fig. 7: Multicolored pinstripe cables.

Fig. 8: 2x2 pinstriped cable.

face each other and the B stitches are at the outside edges of the cable, as in the braid cables of the Pinstriped Cable Pullover.

If you want the same cable across a piece, all the cables should begin with color A and end with color B **(Fig. 6)**. There must be an even number of stitches between cables for true repeating cables. As in classic stranded colorwork, you can add stripes to the background or even change colors often in both background and foreground colors **(Fig. 7)**.

You can create pinstripes that are not 1 but 2 stitches wide **(Fig. 8)**. Like 2x2 rib, the stitch repeat is a multiple of 4, so follow the same rules as for a 2x2 ribble. The smallest cable in this type is 4 over 4 for 8 stitches, or colors A-A-B-B crossed over A-A-B-B. Anything less breaks up the pattern. A 5 over 5 (10 stitches) would mean A-A-B-B-A crossed over A-B-B-A-A; the sets are not the same and the pattern would be broken up.

As long as you can maintain the same number of stitches per color you can even change yarns for a horizontal as well as vertical stirpes.

Working pinstriped cables is like rubbing your stomach and patting your head. You have to do two things at once—maintain the color pattern and cable. While it's not difficult, a certain amount of concentration is involved.

REVERSIBILITY

In almost every method for adding different colored yarns, there is a definite wrong side. Intarsia, mosaic, and stranded knitting are such culprits. The color not being used "floats" on the back, and strands long or short appear. In intarsia, there is a twist at the junction between the yarns. One of the rare exceptions is double knitting, but that adds another layer. A reversible two-color fabric is rare but not impossible. The answer lies in hiding those floats somehow.

As discussed on page 44, the brioche stitch involves catching a horizontal strand or a float on a subsequent row. When a color is not meant to be visible, tuck it away or "hike it up" into the stitch above it. The XOX Raglan Turtleneck uses the one-color equivalent on page 58. There are two methods of working this reversible two-color ribbing, also known as bicolor brioche or two-color tucked rib: with yarnovers or by knitting below.

The yarnover method will not work for Combination or Eastern Uncrossed knitters, who make their purls by wrapping the opposite way and who knit into the back loops of stitches. These knitters are better off using the row-below method that follows.

Note that the "knit-based" rows (the rows that begin and end with k3) have a yarnover before the slipped stitch, but the "purl-based" rows (the rows that begin and end with p3) have a slipped stitch before the yarnover. This allows the yarnovers to loop above "their" respective stitches, almost mimicking the stitch rather than going off on their own as in an eyelet. Also note that yarnovers are worked as if wrapping for a knit stitch on knit-based rows and as if wrapping to purl on purl-based rows.

It takes two rows to complete one full row of bicolor brioche, which is why the rows are lettered as well as numbered. Except for the change in colors, the stitches of Rows 1B and 2A are really the same, and 2B and 3A are the same, too. The resulting fabric has knits in CC and purls in MC on one side and knits in MC and purls in CC on the other. This is a fully reversible two-colored rib.

As for the yarnover method, the knits in the work-below method are in one color and the purls another color on one side, but on the back the knits are of the opposite color and the purls are the first color.

There are no more ungainly floats in either color; the floats are hidden away by tucking (working the yarnover together with a stitch or working into a row below). Tucked or brioche stitches do tend to be squatter and wider stitches than usual.

Although both ways of working this reversible two-colored rib work, I prefer the yarnover technique because the row-below method allows the unused color to bleed through more. This is because instead of a yarnover lying over the stitch, the "float" is worked all the way through.

The floats from yarnovers are shorter and tighter.

The selvedges of 3 garter stitches are a built-in reminder in case you ever lose track of the pattern. Garter stitch works here because it alternates rows of knitting and purling. Although garter is normally worked by knitting all rows, you don't always turn the work after each row in this pattern. Sometimes, you slide the stitches back to the beginning so that the same side faces you. The garter sections at the beginning and end of each row could be expressed as: side A—knit, side A again—purl, side B—purl, side B again—knit. (This two-color garter stitch fabric is also fully reversible.)

If you forget where you are in the pattern, ask yourself: What was the last color I used? Look at the last stitches on the needle. To start a new row, you must work with the opposite color to that of the 3 end stitches. Once you know what color is next, pick up that color and be ready to work. Now what stitch was worked for the end stitches of the last row? These 3 stitches must be worked in the opposite stitch on the next row. If you see knits, you know these 3 stitches must now be purled and vice versa. Once you know what stitch to do at the ends, you know which stitch of the ribbed center portion is either worked into the row below or worked together with a yarnover.

Practice reversible two-colored rib and learn it well enough to work without following the written pattern. Once you can work reversible two-color rib easily, it's not such a stretch to add cables. In order to cable in this pattern, begin a crossing row on the first part of the

Basic Bi-colored Brioche, Yarnover Method

With MC and circular or double-pointed needles, CO 14 stitches.

SET-UP ROW: K3, [k1, p1] 4 times, k3.

Rep last row for 1" (2.5 cm).

ROW 1A: With CC, k3, *k1, yo kwise, sl 1 pwise; rep from * to last 3 sts, k3. Do not turn work; slide sts to beg of row with same side facing.

ROW 1B: With MC, p3, *sl 1, yo pwise, purl next st tog with yo above it; rep from * to last 3 sts, p3. Turn work.

ROW 2A: With CC, p3, *sl 1, yo pwise, purl next st tog with yo above it; rep from * to last 3 sts, p3. Do not turn work; slide sts to beg of row with same side facing.

ROW 2B: With MC, k3, *knit next st tog with yo above it, yo kwise, sl 1; rep from * to last 3 sts, k3. Turn work.

ROW 3A: With CC, k3, *knit next st tog with yo above it, yo kwise, sl 1; rep from * to last 3 sts, k3. Do not turn work; slide sts to beg of row with same side facing.

Rep Rows 1B–3A for patt.

STITCH FILE

Fig. 9: Cabled two-color fisherman's rib.

Basic Bi-colored Brioche, Work-below Method

With MC and circular or double-pointed needles, CO 14 stitches.

SET-UP ROW: K3, [k1, p1] 4 times, k3.

Rep last row for 1" (2.5 cm).

ROW 1A: With CC, k3, *k1, p1; rep from * to last 3 sts, k3. Do not turn work; slide sts to beg of row with same side facing.

ROW 1B: With MC, p3, *k1, purl into the row below next st; rep from * to last 3 sts, p3. Turn work.

ROW 2A: With CC, p3, *k1, purl into the row below next st; rep from * to last 3 sts, p3. Do not turn work; slide sts to beg of row with same side facing.

ROW 2B: With MC, k3, *knit into the row below next st, p1; rep from * to last 3 sts, k3. Turn work.

ROW 3A: With CC, k3, *knit into the row below next st, p1; rep from * to last 3 sts, k3. Do not turn work; slide sts to beg of row with same side facing.

Rep Rows 1B–3A for patt.

row (or any A row). That way, neither color has been worked across yet; both colors should be at the same edge. Make one of the swatches at left and maintain the two-color rib pattern while cabling just the center 8 rib stitches, crossing 4 stitches over 4 **(Fig. 9)**. Work the crossing row every few rows; remember that you need only do it on first half of the row (the A rows).

Like pinstriped cables, these bicolored ribbed reversible cables look sinuous. The colors really underscore and accentuate the movement of the cable. And the two-colored cables look great on either side! Try adding even more texture to an already textured technique with your yarn choices. Try red bouclé with black chenille or yellow silk with green alpaca or . . . you get the idea.

FINISHED MEASUREMENTS

34¾ (36¾, 38½, 40½, 43)" (88.5 [93.5, 98, 103, 109] cm) bust circumference and 24 (24, 24¼, 24¾, 25)" (61 [61, 61.5, 63, 63.5] cm) long, to be worn with standard ease. Sweater shown measures 36¾" (93.5 cm).

YARN

Worsted (Medium #4).

Shown here: Kraemer Summit Hill (100% superwash merino, 230 yd [210 m]/100 g): Onyx #Y1106 (dark blue; A), 3 (3, 3, 4, 4) skeins, and Aquamarine #Y1110 (light blue; B), 2 (3, 3, 3, 4) skeins.

NEEDLES

U.S. sizes 6 and 8 (4 and 5 mm): 24" (60 cm) circular (cir) and set of 4 double-pointed (dpns). Adjust needle sizes if necessary to obtain the correct gauge.

NOTIONS

Stitch markers (m); stitch holder; cable needle (cn); tapestry needle.

GAUGE

23 sts and 22 rnds and rows = 4" (10 cm) in Pinstriped St.
13-st Mirrored Braid cable patt = 2" (5 cm).

PINSTRIPED CABLE
pullover

This pullover features mock darts that follow the lines of traditional princess seams. This effect, produced by mirrored roaming cables, is extremely flattering and slimming. Both the body and sleeves are worked in the round for less seaming. The pinstripe cables on the sleeves extend to the neck as a saddle shoulder.

NOTE

Sweater body and sleeves are worked seamlessly in the round; back and front are divided at underarms and worked back and forth in rows.

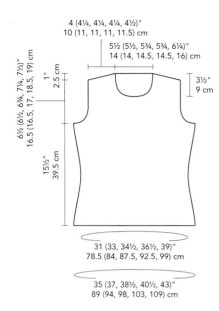

4 (4¼, 4¼, 4¼, 4½)"
10 (11, 11, 11, 11.5) cm

5½ (5½, 5¾, 5¾, 6¼)"
14 (14, 14.5, 14.5, 16) cm

6½ (6½, 6¾, 7¼, 7½)"
16.5 (16.5, 17, 18.5, 19) cm

1"
2.5 cm

3½"
9 cm

15½"
39.5 cm

31 (33, 34½, 36½, 39)"
78.5 (84, 87.5, 92.5, 99) cm

35 (37, 38½, 40½, 43)"
89 (94, 98, 103, 109) cm

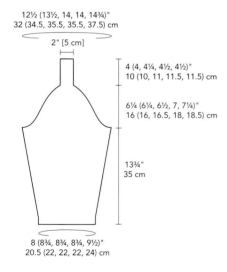

12½ (13½, 14, 14, 14¾)"
32 (34.5, 35.5, 35.5, 37.5) cm

2" [5 cm]

4 (4, 4¼, 4½, 4½)"
10 (10, 11, 11.5, 11.5) cm

6¼ (6¼, 6½, 7, 7¼)"
16 (16, 16.5, 18, 18.5) cm

13¾"
35 cm

8 (8¾, 8¾, 8¾, 9½)"
20.5 (22, 22, 22, 24) cm

PULLOVER

With smaller cir needle and A, CO 206 (218, 226, 238, 254) sts. Join for working in the rnd, being careful not to twist sts. Place marker (pm) for beg of rnd.

Rnd 1: *[K1, p1] 51 (54, 56, 59, 63) times, k1, pm for side "seam," rep from * to end.

Work in patt as established for 1" (2.5 cm).

Body

Change to larger needles.

Rnd 1: *[With A, k1 (K1A); with B, k1 (K1B)] 10 (11, 12, 13, 15) times, pm, work 17 sts of right pinstriped cable, pm, [K1B, K1A] 14 (15, 15, 16, 16) times, K1B, pm, work 17 sts of left pinstriped cable, pm, [K1B, K1A] 10 (11, 12, 13, 15) times; rep from * to end—note 2 consecutive A sts at sides.

Work 4 rnds in patt as established.

Next rnd: (dec rnd 1) *With B, k2tog, work in patt to 2 sts before side m, with A, ssk; rep from * to end—202 (214, 222, 234, 250) sts rem.

Work 4 rnds even in patt as established.

Next rnd: (dec rnd 2) *With A, k2tog, work in patt to 2 sts before side m, with B, ssk; rep from * to end—198 (210, 218, 230, 246) sts rem.

Alternate dec rnds 1 and 2 every 5th rnd 2 more times (4 more dec rnds)—182 (194, 202, 214, 230) sts rem.

Work in patt until piece measures 8½" (21.5 cm).

Next rnd: (inc rnd 1) *Knit first st with B and A, work in patt to 1 st before side marker, knit next st with A and B; rep from * to end—186 (198, 206, 218, 234) sts.

Work 4 rnds even in patt as established.

Next rnd: (inc rnd 2) *Knit first st with A and B, work in patt to 1 st before m, knit next st with B and A; rep from * to end—190 (202, 210, 222, 238) sts total.

Alternate inc rnds 1 and 2 every 5th rnd 2 more times (4 more inc rnds)—206 (218, 226, 238, 254) sts.

Work even in patt until piece measures 15½" (39.5 cm), ending 5 (6, 7, 8, 9) sts before end of last rnd.

Divide for Back and Front

BO 5 (6, 7, 8, 9) sts to beg of rnd, then BO 5 (6, 7, 8, 9) sts, knit to 5 (6, 7, 8, 9) sts before side m, BO 5 (6, 7, 8, 9) sts to side m, BO 5 (6, 7, 8, 9) sts after side marker—93 (97, 99, 103, 109) sts each for Front and Back.

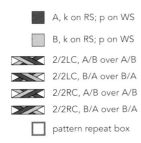

A, k on RS; p on WS

B, k on RS; p on WS

2/2LC, A/B over A/B

2/2LC, B/A over B/A

2/2RC, A/B over A/B

2/2RC, B/A over B/A

pattern repeat box

Pinstriped Body Cables

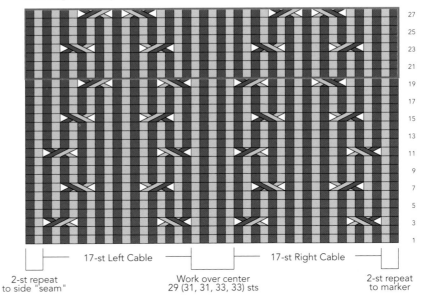

17-st Left Cable   17-st Right Cable

2-st repeat
to side "seam"

Work over center
29 (31, 31, 33, 33) sts

2-st repeat
to marker

Sl first 93 (97, 99, 103, 109) sts to holder or scrap yarn for Front.

Work back and forth in rows over Back sts, maintaining patt as established.

Shape Back Armholes

BO 0 (2, 2, 2, 2) st(s) at beg of next 2 rows—93 (93, 95, 99, 105) sts rem. Dec 1 st at each end of RS row 7 (6, 6, 7, 8) times as foll: K1 (selvedge st) with either color; with color of second st, k2tog, work in patt to last 3 sts, ssk with color of next st, k1 (selvedge st) with either color—2 sts dec'd each RS row; 79 (81, 83, 85, 89) sts rem after last dec.

Work even in patt until armholes measure 6½ (6½, 6¾, 7¼, 7½)" (16.5 [16.5, 17, 18.5, 19] cm).

Shape Shoulders

Working sts into patt, BO 7 sts at beg of next 2 (4, 4, 6, 8) rows, then BO 6 sts at beg of next 6 (4, 4, 2, 0) row(s)—29 (29, 31, 31, 33) sts rem. Place rem sts onto holder.

FRONT

Replace held Front sts on larger cir needle. Reattach yarn and work 1 WS row in patt. Shape armholes as for Back until armholes measure 4 (4, 4¼, 4¾, 5)" (10 [10, 11, 12, 13] cm).

Shape Front Neck

Work 32 (33, 33, 34, 35) sts in patt, place center 15 (15, 17, 17, 19) sts on st holder, join new balls of yarn and work rem 32 (33, 33, 34, 35) sts in patt. Work shoulders separately.

Dec 1 st from each neck edge every RS row 7 times as foll: Left shoulder—work in patt to last 3 sts, ssk with color of next st, k1 (selvedge st) with either color; Right shoulder—k1 (selvedge st) with either color, k2tog with color of second st, work in patt to end. *At the same time* work shoulder shaping as for back when armholes measure 6½ (6½, 6¾, 7¼, 7½)" (16.5 [16.5, 17, 18.5, 19] cm).

SLEEVES

With smaller dpns and A, CO 47 (51, 51, 51, 55) sts. Distribute as evenly as possible over 3 dpns and join for working in the rnd, being careful not to twist sts. Pm for beg of rnd.

Rnd 1: P1, [k1, p1] to end. Work in patt as established for 1" (2.5 cm).

Next row: With larger dpns, *[K1B, K1A] 8 (9, 9, 9, 10) times, K1B*, pm, work 13 sts of Sleeve Cable chart; rep from * to. Working in patt as established, inc in patt as for Body every 4th rnd 2 (2, 12, 12, 12) times, then every 5th rnd 11 (11, 3, 3, 3)

Sleeve Cables

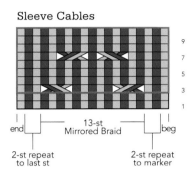

9
7
5
3
1

end
13-st
Mirrored Braid
beg

2-st repeat
to last st

2-st repeat
to marker

- A, k on RS; p on WS
- B, k on RS; p on WS
- 2/2LC, A/B over A/B
- 2/2LC, B/A over B/A
- 2/2RC, A/B over A/B
- 2/2RC, B/A over B/A
- pattern repeat box

times—73 (77, 81, 81, 85) sts.

Work even in patt until sleeve measures 13¾" (35 cm), ending last rnd 5 (6, 7, 8, 9) sts before m for beg of rnd. End with an even number rnd of patt rep.

Shape Cap
BO 5 (6, 7, 8, 9) sts to beg of rnd, BO 5 (6, 7, 8, 9) sts, work in patt to end—63 (65, 67, 65, 67) sts rem. Work back and forth in rows, maintaining patt as established. Work 1 WS row.

BO 0 (2, 2, 2, 2) sts at beg of next 0 (2, 2, 2, 2) row(s)—63 (61, 63, 61, 63) sts rem.

Dec 1 st each end every RS row 8 (7, 7, 11, 11) times as foll: K1 (selvedge st) in either color, k2tog with color of st following next st on left needle, work to last 3 sts, ssk with color of first st, k1 (selvedge st) in either color—47 (47, 49, 39, 41) sts rem.

Next row: (WS; dec row) P1 (selvedge st) with either color, ssp with color of st following next st on left needle, work in patt to last 3 sts, p2tog with color of next st, p1 (selvedge st) in either color. Alternate RS and WS decs 15 (15, 16, 11, 12) more times—15 sts rem.

Saddle Shoulders
Work even in patt until Saddle measures 4 (4¼, 4¼, 4½, 4½)" (10 [11, 11, 11.5, 11.5, 11.5] cm) from last dec. Place rem sts onto holder.

FINISHING

Block pieces to measurements. Set in sleeves and sew sides of saddles to shoulders, using mattress st with 1-st allowance (see Glossary) to cover selvedges.

Neckband
With smaller dpns, A, and RS facing, k15 Right Saddle Shoulder sts, k29 (29, 31, 31, 33) Back Neck Sts, k15 Left Saddle Shoulder sts, pick up and knit (see Glossary) 15 sts evenly along Left Front Neck, k15 (15, 17, 17, 19) Front Neck sts, pick up and knit 15 sts evenly along Right Front Neck—104 (104, 108, 108, 112) sts. Work [k1, p1] rib, with knit over A sts and purl over B sts, for 1" (2.5 cm). Weave in loose ends.

FINISHED MEASUREMENTS
13½" (34.5 cm) wide and 54¼" (138 cm) long.

YARN
Fingering (#1 Super Fine).
Shown here: Skacel/Schulana Mosco (67% viscose, 20% mohair, 13% nylon; 137 yd [125 m]/25 g): Espresso #05 (MC) and Apricot #03 (CC), 5 skeins each.

NEEDLES
U.S. sizes 5 (3.75 mm) and 8 (5.0 mm): circular (cir). Adjust needle sizes if necessary to obtain the correct gauge.

NOTIONS
Stitch markers (m); straight cable needle (cn) or double-pointed needle (dpn); tapestry needle.

GAUGE
16-st cable rep = 2¾" (7 cm).
3-end sts = ½" (1.3 cm)
48-row rep = about 4" (10 cm).

BI-COLOR
brioche stole

This intriguing two-color reversible cable looks almost like moiré fabric. On one side, the knits are of one color and the purls are of the other . . . yet on the other side, the opposite occurs. It takes a bit of concentration, but the results are worth it. Get comfortable with two-color ribbing first (see page 110)—then it's a cinch to cable it.

NOTES

Since this is a reversible piece, use the Russian join (see Glossary) to attach balls of yarn.

Markers indicate garter st side borders. Slip markers (sl m) as you come to them.

If you must rip, just remember that other than the 3 sts at each end of row, every other st will look like 2 sts with the slipped sts and accompanying yarnovers.

Circular (or double-pointed) needles are necessary because sts must be slipped back to the beginning of the row every other row without turning.

stitch guide

4/4LC (4 over 4 left cross): Sl next 4 sts to cn (in patt, it will look like 6 sts, as first and third st have yo above them) and hold in front of work, work 4 sts in patt from left needle, work 4 sts in patt from cn.

4/4RC (4 over 4 right cross): Sl next 4 sts to cn (in patt, it will look like 6 sts, as first and third st have yo above them) and hold in back of work, work 4 sts in patt from left needle, work 4 sts in patt from cn.

Bi-Colored Brioche Rib Pattern

[MULTIPLE OF 2 STS + 6]

ROW 1A: With MC, sl first st purlwise (pwise) with yarn in front (wyf), bring yarn to back and k2, place marker (pm),* k1, yo knitwise (kwise), sl 1 pwise; rep from * to last 3 sts, pm, k2, sl 1 pwise with yarn in back (wyb). Do not turn work; slide sts to beg of row again.

ROW 1B: With CC, p3, * sl 1 pwise wyf, yo pwise, [purl 1 st tog with yo above it]; rep from * to last 3 sts, p3. Turn.

ROW 2A: With MC, sl 1 pwise wyf, p2, * sl 1 pwise wyf, yo pwise, [purl 1 st tog with yo above it]; rep from * to last 3 sts, p2, sl 1 pwise wyf. Do not turn work; slide sts to beg of row again.

ROW 2B: With CC, sl 1 kwise wyb, k2, * [knit 1 st tog with yo above it], yo kwise, sl 1 pwise; rep from * to last 3 sts, k2, sl 1 pwise wyb.

ROW 3A: With MC, sl 1 pwise wyb, k2, *[knit 1 st tog with yo above it] , yo kwise, sl 1 pwise; rep from * to last 3 sts, k2, sl 1 pwise wyib. Do not turn work; slide sts to beg of row again.

Rep Rows 1B–3A for patt.

Bi-Colored Brioche Cable Pattern

(MULTIPLE OF 16 STS + 34)

Work Bi-Colored Brioche Rib patt, ending after Row 2B.

*FIRST CABLE ROW: Continuing to work in Bi-Colored Brioche Rib, work 3 sts in patt, *4/4RC, work 8 sts; rep from * to last 3 sts, work last 3 sts in patt.

NEXT ROW: Work Bi-Colored Brioche Rib Row 1B.

Work in patt for 10 more rows, ending after Bi-Colored Brioche Rib Row 2B.

SECOND CABLE ROW: Continuing to work in Bi-Colored Brioche Rib, work 3 sts in patt, * work 4 sts, 4/4RC, work 4 sts; rep from * to last 3 sts, work last 3 sts in patt.

NEXT ROW: Work Bi-Colored Brioche Rib Row 1B.

Work in patt for 10 more rows, ending after Bi-Colored Brioche Rib Row 2B.

THIRD CABLE ROW: Continuing to work in Bi-Colored Brioche Rib, work 7 sts in patt, * work 8 sts, 4/4RC; rep from * to last 11 sts, work last 11 sts in patt.

NEXT ROW: Work Bi-Colored Brioche Rib Row 1B.

Work in patt for 10 more rows, ending after Bi-Colored Brioche Rib Row 2B.

FOURTH CABLE ROW: Continuing to work in Bi-Colored Brioche Rib, work 3 sts in patt, * work 8 sts, 4/4RC; rep from * to last 15 sts, work last 15 sts in patt.

NEXT ROW: Work Bi-Colored Brioche Rib Row 1B.

Work in patt for 10 more rows, ending after Bi-Colored Brioche Rib Row 2B.

Rep from * for patt.

TIPS

✳ Two rows of knitting are required to complete one pattern row.

✳ Row 1B and Row 2A are the same actions worked in different colors, and Rows 2B and 3A are the same actions worked in different colors.

✳ Note that cables occur on odd-numbered A rows.

✳ Note that for rows with purl sts, each slipped st and yo is worked as [sl 1, yo], but for rows with knit sts, each slipped st and yo is worked as [yo, sl 1].

✳ If you are in doubt of what color to use next, look at the last 3 stitches of the previous row to see which color was used last; as colors alternate rows, this will tell you which color to use next.

✳ If you forget your place in the pattern, with the next row to be worked facing, see whether the first 3 stitches are knitted or purled. This will tell you whether to knit or purl the 3 stitches at each end; they alternate on each row to make the end stitches garter stitch. It will also tell you whether the row is a knit-based or purl-based row—that is, which stitch is "work st tog with yo," which stitch to slip, and if the yarnover is worked knitwise or purlwise.

STOLE

With smaller cir needle, use the chain or crocheted method (see Glossary) to CO 98 sts very loosely.

Work in Bi-Colored Brioche Rib patt for about 1" (2.5 cm), ending after Row 2B.

Change to larger cir needle and begin Bi-Colored Brioche Cable patt.

Work until piece measures about 52¼" (132.5 cm) or desired length, ending after Second Cable Row.

Change to smaller cir and work in regular Bi-Colored Brioche Rib patt for about 1" (2.5 cm), ending with Row 2B. Cut CC, leaving a tail to weave in. With MC, BO very loosely in patt.

Finishing
Block piece to measurements. Weave in ends.

raised wale
cables

Just like traveling stitches, knit wales might sometimes
want to cross with other knit wales, but purl stitches stand
in the way. Rather than travel across the purls, the knit
wales can jump over the purls between them. Shock and
delight your knitting friends with the surprise of a different
cable pattern on either side of your reversible knitting!

THE MAGIC OF RAISED WALES

Raised wale patterns are almost magically reversible; one side cares not what the other is doing. Unlike ribbles (ribbed reversible cables), the cables of the first side have nothing to do with the cables of the second side, yet they are still an integral part of the same single fabric structure. That's all there is to it in order to create mysterious and confounding cables.

Notice that the cable appears on the Row 1 side of the work—the k1s cross over the p2s—yet the other side shows absolutely none of this. Those 2 purl stitches from the crossing side, which are 2 knit stitches on this side, hide that clandestine cable crossing and shield it from our eyes on this side. The cable is only viewable on the other side. (Think of it this way: If I cross my arms in front of me with a hand on each shoulder, you can't see from the back that my arms are crossed. My body is in the way.)

The underlying rib pattern does not need to be uneven like this [k1, p2] rib. In 1x1 rib, the knit wales cross with one another over only 1 purl stitch, not 2.

STITCH FILE

Right and Left Cross Rope Over Two Purl Stitches

To try this exercise, you will need two cable needles.

CO 10 sts.

ROW 1: [K1, p2] 3 times, k1.

ROW 2: [P1, k2] 3 times, p1.

Rep Rows 1 and 2 until piece measures about 1" (2.5 cm), ending after Row 2.

***NEXT ROW:** (right cross row) K1, p2, sl 3 (k1, p2) sts to cn and hold in back, k1 from left needle, sl last 2 (p2) sts from cn back to left needle, hold cn (with rem k1 st) in front, p2 from left needle, k1 from cn, p2, k1.

NEXT ROW: Rep Row 2.

Rep Rows 1 and 2 three more times.

NEXT ROW: (left cross row) K1, p2, sl 1 (k1) to first cn and hold in front, sl 2 (p2) to second cn and hold in back, k1 from left needle, p2 from second cn, k1 from first cn, p2, k1.

NEXT ROW: Rep Row 2.

Rep Rows 1 and 2 three more times.

Rep from * for patt.

FRONT

BACK

Reversible Rope and Braid

CO 25 sts.

ROW 1: [K2, p2] 2 times, k2, [p1, k1] 2 times, p1, [k2, p2] 2 times, k2.

ROW 2: [P2, k2] 2 times, p2, [k1, p1] 2 times, k1, [p2, k2] 2 times, p2.

ROW 3: Sl 4 sts (k2, p2) to cn and hold in back, k2, sl 2 sts (p2) from cn back to left needle, hold rem sts on cn (k2) in front, p2 from left needle, k2 from cn, p2, k2, p1, sl 2 (p1, p1) to cn and hold in back, k1, sl 1 st (p1) from cn back to left needle, hold rem sts on cn (k1) in front, p1 from left needle, k1 from cn, p2, sl 2 sts (k2) to one cn and hold in front, sl 2 sts (p2) to second cn and hold in back, k2 from left needle, p2 from second cn, k2 from first cn.

ROW 4: Rep Row 2.

ROW 5: Rep Row 1.

ROW 6: P2, sl 4 sts (k2, p2) to cn and hold in back, k2, sl 2 sts (p2) from cn back to left needle, hold rem sts on cn (k2) in front, p2 from left needle, k2 from cn, p2, sl 2 (p1, p1) to cn and hold in back, k1, sl 1 st (p1) from cn back to left needle, hold rem sts on cn (k1) in front, p1 from left needle, k1 from cn, p1, k1, p2, sl 2 sts (k2) to one cn and hold in front, sl 2 sts (p2) to second cn and hold in back, k2 from left needle, p2 from second cn, k2 from first cn, p2.

ROWS 7 AND 8: Rep Rows 1 and 2.

ROW 9: K2, p2, sl 2 sts (k2) to one cn and hold in front, sl 2 sts (p2) to second cn and hold in back, k2 from left needle, p2 from second cn, k2 from first cn, p1, sl 1 st (k1) to one cn and hold in front, sl 1 st (p1) to second cn and hold in back, k1 from left needle, p1 from second cn, k1 from first cn, p1, sl 2 sts (k2) to cn and hold in front, sl 2 sts (p2) to second cn and hold in back, k2 from left needle, p2 from second cn, k2 from first cn, p2, k2.

ROW 10: Rep Row 2.

ROW 11: Rep Row 1.

ROW 12: P2, sl 4 sts (k2, p2) to cn and hold in back, k2, sl 2 sts (p2) from cn back to left needle, hold rem sts on cn (k2) in front, p2 from left needle, k2 from cn, p2, k1, p1, sl 1 st (k1) to one cn and hold in front, sl 1 st (p1) to second cn and hold in back, k1 from left needle, p1 from second cn, k1 from first cn, p2, sl 2 sts (k2) to one cn and hold in front, sl 2 sts (p2) to second cn and hold in back, k2 from left needle, p2 from second cn, k2 from first cn, p2.

ROWS 13 AND 14: Rep Rows 1 and 2.

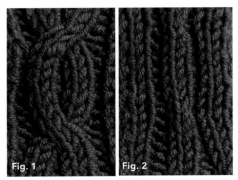

Fig. 1: 2x2 raised wale cables. **Fig. 2:** Back of 2x2 raised wale cables.

In 2x2 rib, a knit wale of 2 stitches crosses with another knit wale of 2 stitches over 2 purl stitches **(Fig. 1)**. Both these cables will look more even on both sides **(Fig. 2)**. Do not go beyond 1 or 2 stitches, however, because there will be too much pull and distortion if the wales have to cross over 3 or more stitches. Don't just take my word for it; try 3x1, 3x2, or 3x3 ribbing for yourself. In the last example, the sets of 3 knit stitches must span the 3 purl sts between them. This is quite a stretch.

For a right cross, slip both the knit and purl wales to a cable needle and hold in back, knit the next stitch(es) from the left needle, slip only the purl stitch(es) from the cable needle back to the left needle, hold the remaining knit stitch(es) on the cable needle in front, purl the stitch(es) from the left needle, knit the stitch(es) from the cable needle.

For a left cross, slip only the knit wale stitch(es) to the first cable needle and hold in front, slip only the purl wale stitch(es) to the second cable needle and hold in back, knit the stitch(es) from the left needle, purl the stitches from the second cable needle, knit the stitches

from the first cable needle.

You can see why I call this the "raise the wales" method. The knit wales come forward to cross on top of the purl wale between them. Unlike regular cables, which show a pinched area of crossed purl on the back, a reversible piece looks like ribbing on the uncabled side.

Reversibility

The example above is pretty reversible, but how do we get cables on both sides? Work cables in this same manner on the other side, too! Using this notion of knits forming cables separately from their background purl stitches, you can actually create different cable patterns on each side of a piece, such as in the Hat and Mittens on page 126.

You now have the beginnings of a three-strand braid, and you've worked both left and right crosses over a differing number of stitches.

To further understand this type of reversible cable, take a look from the top edge **(Fig. 3)**. It's as though you pulled the knitting off the needle. The in-between purl stitches just recess and are not affected by the knit stitches crossing above them and changing positions. The knit stitches are in fact the purl recesses

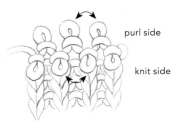

purl side

knit side

Fig. 3: View from the top of ribbing wales crossing. The knit wales can cross without affecting the purl stitches on either side.

of the other side, but you don't see them crossing from there either. You never see the knit stitches from the other side crossing from the present side because they are the purl recesses that fall to the back of the fabric anyway. Look at the different types of cables you can have on each side of a single-layer piece.

Working with Raised Wale Cables

You can use any patterns found in "normal" cables for raised wale cables. The only difference is that instead of crossing a set of knits with an adjacent set of knits, as in a rope cable, there is a set of purls between the crossing knit sets. When setting up the ribbing, keep in mind how many knit wales there are on each side of the fabric; the number of knit wales determines what kind of cable patterns are possible. For instance, three wales present an opportunity to form a braid cable, while seven wales could be a basketweave pattern. A pattern with only two knit wales can create some type of rope cable.

Since there are different cable patterns on each side, it's a good idea to chart the cables for each side. This means that a single piece needs a different chart for each side.

When working reversible raised wale cables, loosen the gauge a lot; I go up at least three needle sizes from the ball band recommendation. Ribs pull in; cables pull in; ribs and cables together pull in exponentially. Try not to work all the cable crosses at once, either. Instead, cross one side's cables on one row and cross the other sides on some other row.

FINISHED MEASUREMENTS

Hat: About 19" (48.5 cm) head circumference (will stretch) and 10" (25.5 cm) tall from brim to crown. *Mittens:* 5½" (14 cm) cuff circumference, 7¾" (19.5 cm) palm circumference, and length to fit; sample measures 6" (15 cm) from cuff to tip of fingers.

YARN

Worsted weight (Medium #4).

Shown here: Cascade Indulgence (70% super-fine alpaca, 30% angora 123 yd [112 m]/50 g): Red #524, 2 skeins for hat, 1 skein for mittens. *Note:* The mittens require almost exactly 1 skein. If you plan to make only the mittens, an extra skein may be necessary for swatching or any modifications to size or gauge.

NEEDLES

U.S. size 7 (4.5 mm): 16" (40 cm) circular (cir) (for hat only) and set of 5 double-pointed (dpns).

NOTIONS

8 stitch markers (m); 2 cable needles (cn); smooth waste yarn to use as stitch holder; tapestry needle.

GAUGE

Hat: 24 sts and 32 rnds = 4" (10 cm) in St st in the rnd.
Mittens: 22 sts and 29 rnds = 4" (10 cm) in St st in the rnd.

REVERSIBLE CUFFS
hat & mittens

These mittens and hat have reversible cuffs for warmth and variety: one side has thicker rope cables and the other side features more delicate basketweave cables. These reversible cables are worked in the round, never turning the work. See the instructions on page 125 for crossing purl wales behind the knit wales to work the crosses of both sides with only one side facing.

NOTE

Since this is a reversible piece using animal fiber, use the spit splice (see Glossary) to join new yarn.

stitch guide

1/1RC (1/1 Right Cross): Sl next knit st and 2 purl sts to cn and hold in back, k1 from left needle, sl 2 purl sts from cn back to left needle, hold cn with rem st in front, p2 from left needle, k1 from cn.

2/2RC (2/2 Right Cross): Sl 2 purl sts to cn and hold in back, sl next knit st to second cn and hold in front, p2 from left needle, k1 from front cn, p2 from back cn.

1/1LC (1/1 Left Cross): Sl 1 knit st to cn and hold in front, sl next 2 purl sts to second cn and hold in back, k1 from left needle, p2 from back cn, k1 from front cn.

2/2LC (2/2 Left Cross): Sl 2 purl sts and 1 knit st to cn and hold in front, p2 from left needle, sl knit st from cn back to left needle, hold cn in back, k1 from left needle, p2 from cn.

Cable Pattern

RNDS 1 AND 2: *K1, p2; rep from * to end.

RND 3: *1/1 RC, p2; rep from * to end.

RNDS 4 AND 5: Rep Rnd 1.

RND 6: *K1, 2/2 RC; rep from * to end.

RNDS 7 AND 8: Rep Rnd 1.

RND 9: Sl first st of rnd to end of rnd (move 1 st right), *p2, 1/1 LC; rep from * to end, sl last st back to beg of rnd (move 1 st left).

RNDS 10 AND 11: Rep Rnd 1.

RND 12: * K1, 2/2 LC; rep from * to end.

Rep Rnds 1–12 for pattern.

Cable Pattern

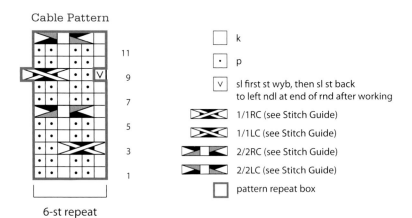

☐	k
·	p
V	sl first st wyb, then sl st back to left ndl at end of rnd after working
⬚	1/1RC (see Stitch Guide)
⬚	1/1LC (see Stitch Guide)
⬚	2/2RC (see Stitch Guide)
⬚	2/2LC (see Stitch Guide)
☐	pattern repeat box

6-st repeat

HAT

Crown

Make slipknot with tail and place on left needle.

Rnd 1: [K1, yo] into single st 4 times—8 sts. Arrange sts evenly over 4 dpns and join for working in the rnd, being careful not to twist sts. (Change to cir needle when there are enough sts to work comfortably.)

Rnd 2 and all even rnds to Rnd 22: Knit.

Rnd 3: *K1, M1 (see Glossary), place marker (pm); rep from * to end—16 sts.

Rnd 5 and all odd-numbered rnds to Rnd 23: *Knit to m, M1, sl m; rep from * to end—8 sts inc'd; 96 sts after Rnd 23.

Rnds 24 and 25: Knit.

Rnd 26: Rep Rnd 5.

Rnds 27–32: Rep Rnds 24–26 twice—120 sts after Rnd 32.

Remove all m except for one indicating beg of rnd. Work even in St st until hat measures 4½" (11.5 cm) from CO.

Brim

Work Rnds 1–12 of Cable patt 3 times, then rep Rnds 1–3 of Cable patt.

BO loosely in patt. Tighten beg slipknot and fasten off tail securely inside. Weave in loose ends.

MITTENS

Cuff

CO 42 sts loosely. Divide as evenly as possible over 4 dpns and join for working in the rnd, being careful not to twist sts.

Work Rnds 1–12 of Cable patt 2 times, then rep Rnds 1–4 of cable patt. Work in St st for 6 rnds or to desired base of thumb.

Thumb gusset

Rnd 1: K20, pm, M1, k2, M1, pm, k20—44 sts.

Rnd 2 and all even rnds to Rnd 12: Knit.

Rnd 3 and all odd-numbered rnds to Rnd 13: Knit to m, sl m, M1, knit to m, M1, sl m, knit to end—2 sts inc'd; 56 sts at the end of Rnd 13.

Rnd 14: K20, sl 16 sts to scrap yarn holder, k20.

Hand

Work even in St st over 40 hand sts for 14 rnds or to desired length to tip of little finger.

Rnd 1: (dec rnd) *Pm, ssk, k16, k2tog; rep from * to end—36 sts rem.

Rnds 2 and 4: Knit.

Rnd 3: (dec rnd) *Ssk, knit to 2 sts before m, k2tog, sl m; rep from * to end—4 sts dec'd; 32 sts rem.

Rnds 5–8: Rep Rnd 3—16 sts rem after Rnd 8.

Sl first 8 sts to 1 dpn and last 8 sts to another dpn. Cut yarn, leaving an 8" (20.5 cm) tail. Use Kitchener st (see Glossary) to graft sts or turn piece with WS out and BO using 3-needle method (see Glossary).

Thumb

Arrange 16 held thumb sts on 3 dpns. Rejoin yarn.

With RS facing, work St st for 8 rnds or to ½" (1.3 cm) from tip of thumb.

Next rnd: (dec rnd) *Ssk, k4, k2tog; rep from * to end—12 sts.

Next rnd: Knit.

Rep last 2 rows once, then rep dec rnd once more—4 sts rem.

Cut yarn, leaving a 7" (18 cm). Draw tail through rem sts, pull tight to snug, and fasten off securely on the WS.

phony cables

When is a cable not a cable? When stitches don't actually cross or change positions. There are several ways to create the look of a cable without actually working a cable.

A horizontal bar across a group of stitches or a puckering of the fabric's texture can give the appearance of a cable without actually rearranging stitches. In one color or two, reversible or not, these phonies are often quicker to execute than the real cables. Avoiding a cable needle can be appealing!

SLIPPED STITCH MOCK CABLES

One mock cable technique employs a passed-over slipstitch to emulate a cable crossing. By passing this first stitch over the last two almost as if to bind off, however, a stitch is lost. Not to worry—you can get it back later. In essence, this is a form of ribbing in which one of the stitches in the knit wale gives the look of a cable. Create a lacy effect by replacing the lost stitch with a yarnover. One interesting hybrid, which is barely lacy, does not change the number of stitches at any time. The techniques can be combined with a half-drop by staggering the row on which the stitch is slipped and passed over. You could even use this idea for reversible wide-rib mock cables by setting up a pattern with even numbers of knits and purls, then passing knit stitches over on both sides.

Another variation on slipping a stitch for

STITCH FILE

Basic Mock Cable

CO 29 sts (or a multiple of 4 + 1).

ROW 1: (RS) [P1, k3] to last st, p1.

ROW 2: [K1, p3] to last st, k1.

ROW 3: (cable row) [P1, sl 1 kwise wyb, k2, pass slipped st over (psso) last 2 sts by lifting slipped st over and dropping off the end of the right needle to form a bar that resembles a cable-crossing] to last st, p1. There is one fewer st in each cable.

ROW 4: [K1, p1, purl into the horizontal bar formed by sl st of prev row, p1] to last st, k1. The original number of sts is restored.

Rep Rows 1–4 for patt.

Eyelet Baby "Cable"

CO 29 sts (or a multiple of 4 + 1).

ROW 1: (RS) [P1, k3] to last st, p1.

ROW 2: [K1, p3] to last st, k1.

ROW 3: (cable row) [P1, sl 1 kwise wyb, k2, pass slipped st over (psso) last 2 sts by lifting slipped st over and dropping off the end of the right needle to form a bar that resembles a cable-crossing] to last st, p1. There is one fewer st in each cable.

ROW 4: [K1, p1, yo pwise, p1] to last st, end k1. The original number of sts is restored.

Rep Rows 1–4 for patt.

Hybrid Mock Cable

CO 29 sts (or a multiple of 4 + 1)

ROW 1: (RS) [P1, k3] to last st, p1.

ROW 2: [K1, p3] to last st, k1.

ROW 3: (cable row) [P1, sl 1 kwise wyb, k1, yo, k1, pass slipped st over (psso) last 3 sts (including yo) by lifting slipped st over and dropping off the end of the right needle to form a bar that resembles a cable-crossing] to last st, p1.

ROW 4: Rep Row 2.

Rep Rows 1–4 for patt.

STITCH FILE

a mock cable is used on the hood of the Three Fakes Hoodie (page 146). Worked over ribbing, this version is reversible, and like the hybrid version it doesn't require adding a stitch on a subsequent row. Instead of slipping a knit stitch and passing it over, work a yarnover to pass over worked stitches. The yarnover is an added stitch, but it's lost again when it is passed over, so the stitch count doesn't change. The hood uses a yarnover passed over 4 stitches; you can even try passing the yarnover over 6 stitches, but it's a little tricky. Try it in stockinette instead of ribbing for a nonreversible phony cable.

CLUSTER STITCHES

Unlike the mock cable technique above, cluster stitches do involve a cable needle, though not in the traditional way. Wrapping the yarn around the base of several stitches creates the sense of a cable. You can work more rows between wrapping rows or add stitches to the knit and purl areas. To make this reversible, work a ribbing pattern with an equal number of knit and purl stitches; try [k1, p1] rib (multiple of 2 stitches) or [k2, p2] rib (multiple of 4 stitches).

Cluster Stitches with a Half-drop

CO 26 sts (or a multiple of 5 + 1).

ROW 1: (RS) [P1, k4] to last st, p1.

ROW 2 AND ALL WRONG-SIDE ROWS: [K1, p4] to last st, k1.

ROW 3: (first cable row) *P1, k4, slip 4 sts just worked to cn, wrap working yarn around the base of 4 sts on cn counter-clockwise 3 times, sl 4 sts on cn back to right needle, p1, k4; rep from * 1 time, k4, sl 4 st from right needle to cn and wrap 3 times, replace 4 cn sts on right needle, p1.

ROW 5: (second cable row) *P1, k4, p1, k4, sl 4 sts just worked to cn and wrap 3 times, sl 4 sts on cn back to right needle; rep from * 1 time, p1, k4, p1.

ROW 6: Rep Row 2.

Rep Rows 3–6 for patt.

TROMPE L'OEIL MOCK CABLES

A fun way to make a faux cable is to use what the French call *trompe l'oeil* (literally, trick the eye). This false cable is really a picture of a cable done in stranded color-work. Try working this in knits and purls instead of colors for a textured phony —work the color A stitches in stockinette and the color B stitches in reverse stockinette.

OTHER CREATIVE IDEAS

For a trim, belt, or purse handle (as in the Two-Colored Handbag on page 136), try making two strips of fabric and passing them through one another. I did this in two colors, but you can try this with just one. This technique creates a fully reversible two-color cable look. The strap for the bag is worked entirely in stockinette.

  Another reversible phony cable method also involves a cable needle, such as the cluster stitch. However, this method involves rotating the stitches on the cable needle 180° or a half turn, then returning the stitches onto the needle. Worked in a ribbing pattern, this can be reversible, or try a nonreversible version in stockinette. Try it in seed stitch as well for other reversible cable textures. The Turnaround Stole on page 142 uses this technique.

STITCH FILE

Stranded Trompe l'Oeil Cable

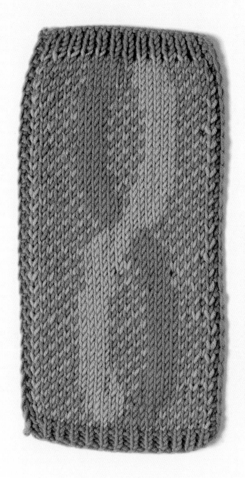

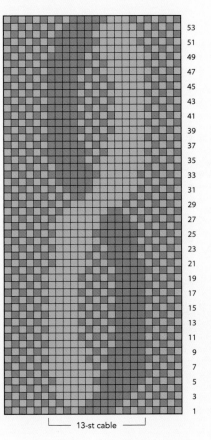

13-st cable

STITCH FILE

Simpler Stranded Trompe l'Oeil Cable

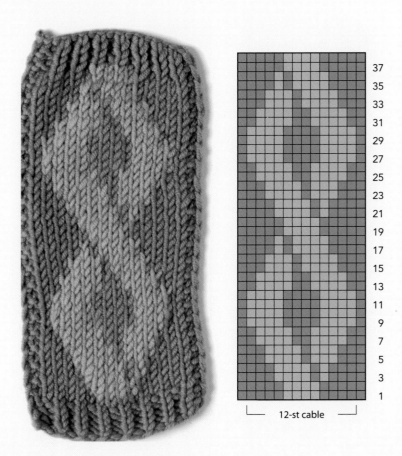

37
35
33
31
29
27
25
23
21
19
17
15
13
11
9
7
5
3
1

12-st cable

The Three-Fakes Hoodie on page 146 is an exercise in three—count 'em, three!—different ways to create cable-like effects, two of which are reversible. The hood uses the slipped-stitch-yarnover method described on page 132. The reversible two-colored trim described on page 153 could be worked in only one color, but it requires two separate knitted strands. Use it to trim all kinds of edges. Pick up a multiple of 3 stitches initially for a flat piece and a multiple of 6 stitches for pieces in the round.

The final and most noticeable false cable is made up of I-cord passing through fabric, in this case stockinette stitch. Eyelets are placed so that when I-cord is threaded through them in a particular order, it imparts the illusion of cables. You could even turn this non-reversible method into a reversible one by threading I-cords through eyelets in a reversible piece such as ribbing, garter, or seed stitch.

TWO-COLORED
handbag

The strap of this purse mirrors the cables of the body. The straps are actually faux two-colored cables, while the bag body features the real deal. See how fun and easy this deceptive cabled-strap pattern is! Fool all your knitting friends into thinking you did a lot more work than you really did. Use the faux-cable technique for a matching belt.

FINISHED SIZE

10" (25.5 cm) wide, 7" (18 cm) tall, and 1" (2.5 cm) side and bottom; 33" (84 cm) strap.

YARN

Sportweight (Fine #2).
Shown here: Reynolds Cool Cotton (90% cotton, 10% cool steel; 114 yd [104 m/50 g]) Absinthe #3 (yellow; A) and Slate Blue #19 (B), 2 skeins each.

NEEDLES

U.S. size 5 (3.75 mm): 16" (40 cm) circular (cir), set of four or five 12" (30.5 cm) and set of four or five 5" (12.5 cm) double-pointed (dpn) . Adjust needle size if necessary to obtain the correct gauge.

NOTIONS

Stitch markers (m); scrap yarn or stitch holders; cable needle (cn); one 9" (23 cm) zipper in a coordinating color; sewing needle and sewing thread to match zipper; lining fabric (optional); tapestry needle.

GAUGE

Six 8-st reps of Cable patt (48 sts) and five 8-rnd reps (40 rnds) = 5" (12.5 cm).
8 sts of Bottom patt (without selvedges) = 1" (2.5 cm).

NOTE

Bottom of tote is worked first, then sts are picked up from all sides and worked upward in the round.

Body Cable Pattern

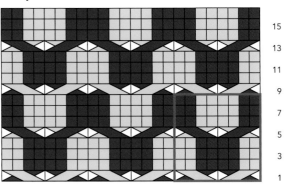

15
13
11
9
7
5
3
1

8-st repeat

☐ Absinthe (yellow; A)

■ Slate Blue (B)

2A/2B RC (see Stitch Guide)

2A/2B LC (see Stitch Guide)

2B/2A RC (see Stitch Guide)

2B/2A LC (see Stitch Guide)

stitch guide

2A/2B RC (2 A sts over 2 B sts Right Cross): Sl 2 (B) sts to cn and hold in back of work, with A, k2 (A), with B, k2 (B) from cn.

2A/2B LC (2 A sts over 2 B sts Left Cross): Sl 2 (A) sts to cn and hold in front of work, with B, k2 (B), with A, k2 (A) from cn.

2B/2A RC (2 B sts over 2 A sts Right Cross): Sl 2 (A) sts to cn and hold in back of work, with B, k2 (B), with A, k2 (A) from cn.

2B/2A LC (2 B sts over 2 A sts Left Cross): Sl 2 (B) sts to cn and hold in front of work, with A, k2 (A), with B, k2 (B) from cn.

Body Cable Pattern

(MULTIPLE OF 8 STS)

RND 1: *2A/2B RC, 2A/2B LC; rep from * to end.

RNDS 2–4: *With A, k2, with B, k4, with A, k2; rep from * to end.

RND 5: *2B/2A RC, 2B/2A LC; rep from * to end.

RNDS 6–8: *With B, k2, with A, k4, with B, k2; rep from * to end.

Rep Rnds 1–8 for patt.

TOTE

Bottom

Note: The bottom is worked outward in two directions from the CO.

With shorter dpns and A or B, use the chain or crochet method (see Glossary) to CO 10 sts.

FIRST END

Row 1: (RS) With B, k3, with A, k4, with B, k3.

Row 2: With A, p1, with B, p2, with A, p4, with B, p2, with A, p1.

Row 3: (first crossing row) With B, k1, 2A/2B RC, 2A/2B LC, with B, k1.

Rows 4 and 6: With A, p3, with B, p4, with A, p3.

Row 5: With B, k1, with A, k2, with B, k4, with A, k2, with B, p1.

Row 7: (second crossing row) With B, k1, 2B/2A RC, 2B/2A LC, with B, k1.

Row 8: Rep Row 2.

Rep Rows 1–8 three more times, then work Rows 1–7 once more, ending after a RS row (39 rows total). Cut yarns, leaving tails to weave in, and keep live sts on dpn.

SECOND END

With RS facing, pick up and knit (see Glossary) 10 sts along CO edge with same yarn as beg. Work as for First Side, but do not cut yarns.

Body

SET UP FOR BODY

With RS facing, rotate bottom piece 90°. With 1 longer dpn, pick up and knit 96 sts evenly along one long side of bottom in color patt as foll: [2B, 4A, 2B] to end, place marker (pm). (To pick up and knit 96 sts, *pick up and knit 1 st in each row 3 times, then pick up and knit 2 sts in next row; rep from * until 96 sts have been worked.) With shorter dpn, held sts at end of strip, and B, k2tog, k1, with A, k4, with B, k1, ssk, pm. Pick up and knit 96 sts along other side of bottom strip and work held sts at other end of strip as for the first half, placing markers to indicate end of each side—208 sts. Join for working in the rnd.

SIDES

With RS facing, work Body Cable patt until piece measures 6½" (16.5 cm) from picked up sts, ending after Rnd 3. Change to cir needles when desired.

TOP TRIM

Next rnd: Maintaining color patt as established, sl 1 st purlwise (pwise), k1, [p1, k2tog, p1, k1, p2tog, k1] to last 2 sts, k1, purl last st of rnd tog with first st of rnd, replace m after last p2tog—156 sts rem.
Work [k1, p1] in color patt as established for 1 row.

Next rnd: Maintaining color patt as established, k1, [p1, k1] 34 times, p1, sl1, k2tog, psso, p1, k1, p1, sl1, k2tog, psso, p1, [k1, p1] 34 times, sl1, k2tog, psso, p1, k1, p1, end 2 sts before end marker—150 sts rem. Cut A, leaving a tail to weave in.

Next rnd: With B, work in patt and *at the same time* BO as foll: sl 2 tog kwise, k1, p2sso, *[sl 2 tog kwise, k1, p2sso, k1, p1, k1] 11 times, [sl 2 tog kwise, k1, p2sso, k1] twice; rep from * once, sl 2 tog kwise, k1, p2sso, k1, sl 2 tog kwise, k1, p2sso. Cut B and draw through last st to fasten off.

Straps

A STRAP

With A and shorter dpn, CO 9 sts.

Row 1 and all odd-numbered rows: (WS) Purl.

Row 2: Knit.

Row 4: (RS; eyelet row): K4, yo, k2tog, k3.

Rows 6 and 8: Knit.

Rep Rows 1–8 twenty-eight times, then work Rows 1–7 once more—piece measures about 35½" (90 cm) with 29 eyelets. Cut yarn, leaving a 12" (30.5 cm) tail. Place sts on scrap yarn.

B STRAP

With B and shorter dpn, CO 9 sts.

Row 1 and all odd-numbered rows: (WS) Purl.

Rows 2, 4, and 6: Knit.

Row 8: (RS; eyelet row) K4, yo, k2tog, k3.

Rep Rows 1–8 twenty-eight times, then work Rows 1–7 once more—piece measures about 35½" (90 cm) with 29 eyelets. Cut yarn, leaving a 12" (30.5 cm) tail. Place sts on scrap yarn to hold.

JOIN STRAPS

Lace straps through each other as foll (see diagram below): With RS of each strip facing and CO of each strap at bottom, lay A strip on top of B strip. Pin or clip CO edges tog, and work with top edges (where sts are on hold).

Beg at bottom edge of straps, push top edge of B strap up through bottom eyelet of A strap and pull until taut; B strap is now on top.

Push top edge of A strap up through bottom eyelet of B strap and pull until taut; A strap is now on top.

*Push top edge of B strap up through next eyelet of A strap and pull until taut; B strap is now on top.

Push top edge of A strap up through next eyelet of B strap and pull until taut; A strap is now on top.

Rep from * until A strap has passed through 14th eyelet of B strap and A strap is on top.

*Push top edge of A strap down through next eyelet of B strap and pull until taut; B strap is now on top.

Push top edge of B strap down through next eyelet of A strap and pull until taut; A strap is now on top.

Rep from * until straps have passed through all eyelets; A strap is on top.

Replace held sts on 2 separate shorter dpns. With RS facing, hold A needle in front of B needle; with third needle, *k1 from A needle and 1 st from B tog. Rep from * to end. Use the 3-needle method (see Glossary) to join and BO straps.

Finishing

Sew CO end of B strap to WS of A strap. With tail threaded in tapestry needle, use Kitchener st (see Glossary) to sew end of strap to one side of bag below top trim, matching colors. Sew BO end of strap to other side of bag. Weave in all ends. With sewing needle and matching thread, sew in zipper (see Glossary). Line if desired.

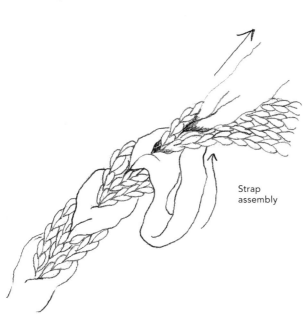

Strap assembly

TURNAROUND
stole

This stole demonstrates yet another reversible faux cable. Instead of crossing sets of stitches over one another, the rib stitches placed on a cable needle on a cable needle do a 180° turn. The brushed baby alpaca yarn makes the piece weightless yet warm. Work fewer repeats of the stitch pattern for a smaller scarf-sized version or make a larger version for a whole afghan.

FINISHED SIZES
18½" (47 cm) wide and 57" (145 cm) long.

YARN
Chunky (Bulky #5).
Shown here: Plymouth's Baby Alpaca Brush (80% baby alpaca, 20% acrylic; 110 yd [101 m]/50 g): Teal #17, 8 skeins.

NEEDLES
U.S. size 10 (6.0 mm). Adjust needle size if necessary to obtain the correct gauge.

NOTIONS
Stitch markers (m); straight cable needle (cn) or double-pointed needle (dpn); tapestry needle.

GAUGE
24 sts (or four 6-st cables) and 18 rows = 4" (10 cm) in ribbed cable patt.

NOTES
Since this is a reversible piece worked in an animal fiber, use the spit-splice (see Glossary) to join balls of yarn.
Markers indicate garter st side borders. Slip markers (sl m) as you come to them.

stitch guide

LTn (left turn): Sl 6 sts to cn, turn 180° clockwise (or turn the right point of the cn toward you until it faces left), work [k1, p1] rib from cn.

RTn (right turn): Sl 6 sts to cn, turn 180° counterclockwise (or turn the right point of the cn away from you until it faces left), work [k1, p1] rib from cn.

STOLE

CO 108 sts.

Row 1 and all odd-numbered rows: Sl 1 purlwise (pwise) with yarn in front (wyf), bring yarn to back, k2, place marker (pm), [k1, p1] to last 3 sts, pm, k3.

Rows 2 and 4: Rep Row 1.

Row 6: Sl 1 pwise wyf, bring yarn to back, k2, *LTn, [k1, p1] 3 times; rep from * to last 9 sts, LTn, k3.

Rows 8 and 10: Rep Row 1.

Row 12: Sl 1 pwise wyf, bring yarn to back, k2, *[k1, p1] 3 times, RTn; rep from * to last 9 sts, [k1, p1] 3 times, K3.

Rep Rows 1–12 until piece measures 56" (142 cm) or desired length, ending after Row 6 or Row 12. Rep Row 1 four more times. BO very tightly in patt.

Finishing

Block piece to measurements. Weave in ends.

FINISHED SIZES

35 (37, 39½, 42, 44½)" (89 [94, 100.5, 106.5, 113] cm) bust circumference and 20¼ (20¼, 20½, 20¾, 21¼)" (51.5 [51.5, 52, 52.5, 54] cm) long (measured without hood); to fit with standard ease. Hoodie shown measures 37" (94 cm).

YARN

DK (Light #3).
Shown here: Filatura di Crosa Zara (100% superwash merino; 137 yd [125m]/50 g) Crimson #1493 (MC), 11 (12, 13, 15, 16) balls, and Charcoal Gray #1468 (CC), 3 (3, 4, 4) skeins.

NEEDLES

U.S. size 7 (4.5 mm): 24" (60 cm) circular (cir) and set of 5 double-pointed (dpns). Adjust needle size if necessary to obtain the correct gauge.

NOTIONS

Stitch markers (m); tapestry needle.

GAUGE

20 sts and 29 rows = 4" (10 cm) in St st after steam blocking and hanging.
30 sts and 28 rows = 4" (10 cm) in ribbed mock cable patt.

THREE-FAKES
hoodie

This cozy sweater demonstrates three different methods for creating the illusion of knitted cables without actually cabling: The largest motif uses I-cord woven through eyelets for a mock-cable effect. The reversible phony cable on the hood, which requires no cable needle, resembles smocking. The two-color edging is applied during finishing.

NOTES

Since hood is reversible, use the Russian join (see Glossary) to attach balls of yarn.
Hood is worked by extending Back piece, then sts are picked up and worked sideways.

stitch guide

Right Lace Pattern

(6 STS)

ROW 1: (RS) K4, ssk, yo.

ROWS 2–8: Work in St st.

ROW 9: Yo, k2tog, k2, ssk, yo.

ROWS 10–16: Work in St st.

Rep Rows 9–16 for patt.

LAST ROW: (RS) Yo, k2tog, k4.

Right Sleeve & Center Lace Pattern

(11 STS)

ROW 1: (RS) K3, yo, k2tog, k6.

ROWS 2–8: Work in St st.

ROW 9: K6, ssk, yo, k3.

ROWS 10–16: Work in St st.

ROW 17: K3, yo, k2tog, k4, ssk, yo.

ROWS 18–24: Work in St st.

ROW 25: Yo, k2tog, k4, ssk, yo, k3.

ROWS 26–32: Work in St st.

Rep Rows 17–32 for patt.

2ND-TO-LAST LACE ROW [RS]: K9, ssk, yo.

VERY LAST LACE ROW [RS]: Yo, k2tog, k9.

Left Lace Pattern

(6 STS)

ROW 1: (RS): Yo, k2tog, k4.

ROWS 2–8: Work in St st.

ROW 9: Yo, k2tog, k2, ssk, yo.

ROWS 10–16: Work in St st.

Rep Rows 9–16.

LAST ROW: (RS) K4, ssk, yo.

Left Sleeve Lace Pattern

(11 STS)

ROW 1 [RS]: K6, ssk, yo, k3.

ROWS 2–8: Work in St st.

ROW 9: K3, yo, k2tog, k6.

ROWS 10–16: Work in St st.

ROW 17: Yo, k2tog, k4, ssk, yo, k3.

ROWS 18–24: Work in St st.

ROW 25: K3, yo, k2tog, k4, ssk, yo.

ROWS 26–32: Work in St st.

Rep Rows 17–32 for patt.

2ND-TO-LAST LACE ROW [RS]: Yo, k2tog, K9.

VERY LAST LACE ROW [RS]: K9, ssk, yo.

Mock Cable Pattern

(MULTIPLE OF 8 STS)

ROW 1 AND ALL WS ROWS: P2 (selvedge sts), [k1, p1] to last 2 sts, p2 (selvedge sts).

ROW 2: (RS) K2 (selvedge sts), yo, [k1, p1] twice; use tip of left needle to lift yo over 4 sts just worked (sl yo), *[k1, p1] twice, yo, [k1, p1] twice, sl yo; rep from * to last 2 sts, k2 (selvedge sts).

ROWS 4 AND 8: K2, [k1, p1] to last 2 sts, k2.

ROW 6: K2, [k1, p1] twice, *yo, [k1, p1] twice, sl yo, [k1, p1] twice; rep from * to last 2 sts, k2.

Rep Rows 1–8 for patt.

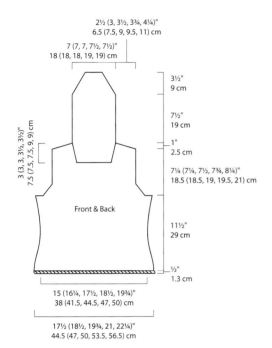

2½ (3, 3½, 3¾, 4¼)"
6.5 (7.5, 9, 9.5, 11) cm

7 (7, 7, 7½, 7½)"
18 (18, 18, 19, 19) cm

3½"
9 cm

7½"
19 cm

1"
2.5 cm

3 (3, 3, 3½, 3½)"
7.5 (7.5, 7.5, 9, 9) cm

7¼ (7¼, 7½, 7¾, 8¼)"
18.5 (18.5, 19, 19.5, 21) cm

Front & Back

11½"
29 cm

½"
1.3 cm

15 (16¼, 17½, 18½, 19¾)"
38 (41.5, 44.5, 47, 50) cm

17½ (18½, 19¾, 21, 22¼)"
44.5 (47, 50, 53.5, 56.5) cm

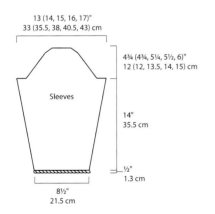

13 (14, 15, 16, 17)"
33 (35.5, 38, 40.5, 43) cm

4¾ (4¾, 5¼, 5½, 6)"
12 (12, 13.5, 14, 15) cm

Sleeves

14"
35.5 cm

½"
1.3 cm

8½"
21.5 cm

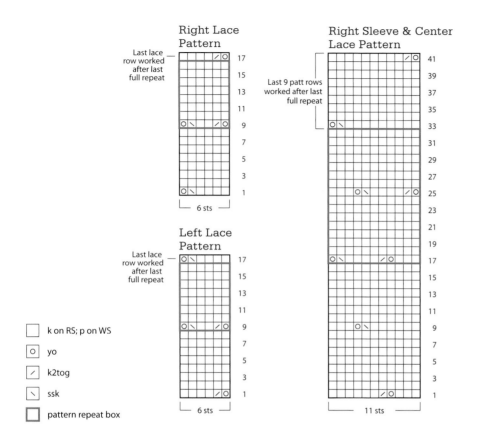

Right Lace Pattern

Last lace row worked after last full repeat

17 15 13 11 9 7 5 3 1

6 sts

Right Sleeve & Center Lace Pattern

Last 9 patt rows worked after last full repeat

41 39 37 35 33 31 29 27 25 23 21 19 17 15 13 11 9 7 5 3 1

11 sts

Left Lace Pattern

Last lace row worked after last full repeat

17 15 13 11 9 7 5 3 1

6 sts

□ k on RS; p on WS
O yo
✓ k2tog
＼ ssk
□ pattern repeat box

BACK

With MC and cir needle, CO 89 (95, 101, 107, 113) sts.

Set-up row: (WS) P19 (20, 21, 22, 23), place marker (pm), p6, pm, p14 (16, 18, 20, 22), pm, p11, pm, p14 (16, 18, 20, 22), pm, p6, pm, p19 (20, 21, 22, 23).

Row 1: K19 (20, 21, 22, 23), work Right Lace Patt, k14 (16, 18, 20, 22), work Center Lace Patt, k14 (16, 18, 20, 22), work Left Lace Patt, k19 (20, 21, 22, 23). Work in patt as established for 6 more rows.

Shape Waist

Next row: (RS; dec row) K2, k2tog, work in patt to last 4 sts, ssk, k2—2 sts dec'd. Rep dec row every 6 rows 5 more times—77 (83, 89, 95, 101) sts rem. Work even in patt for 7 rows; piece measures about 6¼" (16 cm).

Shape Bust

Next row: (RS; inc row) K2, M1 (see Glossary), work in patt to last 2 sts, M1, k2—2 sts inc'd. Rep inc row every 6 rows 5 more times—89 (95, 101, 107, 113) sts.

Work even in patt until piece measures about 13" (33 cm), ending after a WS row.

Shape Armholes

BO 6 (7, 7, 8, 8) sts at beg of next 2 rows—77 (81, 87, 91, 97) sts rem.

Next row: (RS; dec row) K2, k2tog, work in patt to last 4 sts, ssk, k2—2 sts dec'd. Rep dec row every RS row 6 (6, 7, 6, 7) more times—63 (67, 71, 77, 81) sts rem. Work even in patt until armholes measure 8 (8, 8¼, 8½, 9)" (20.5 [20.5, 21, 21.5, 23] cm), ending after a WS row and end Left and Right Lace Patts rep, then work last 9 rows as shown on charts before reaching shoulders.

Shape Shoulders

BO 5 (5, 6, 7, 7) sts at beg of next 2 (2, 6, 2, 2) rows, then 4 (6, 0, 6, 8) sts at beg of next 2 (2, 0, 2, 2) rows, then 5 (5, 0, 7, 7) sts at beg of next 2 (2, 0, 2, 2) rows—35 (35, 35, 37, 37) sts rem.

Hood

Work even in patt, maintaining Center Lace Patt, until piece measures 7½" (19 cm) from last shoulder BO row, ending after a WS row.

Next row: (RS; dec row) K2, k2tog, work in patt to last 4 sts, ssk, k2—2 sts dec'd. Rep dec row every 4th row 4 more times, ending Center Lace Patt with a complete patt rep, then rep dec row every RS row 4 more times and work last 9 rows of Center Lace Patt.

BO rem 17 (17, 17, 19, 19) sts.

FRONT

Work as for Back until armhole measures 4 (4, 4¼, 4, 4½)" (10 [10, 11, 10, 11.5] cm), ending Center Lace Patt with a complete patt rep. Work last 9 rows of Center Lace Patt chart; piece measures 5¼ (5¼, 5½, 5¼, 5¾)" (13.5 [13.5, 14, 13.5, 14.5] cm) inches from beg of Armhole, ending after a WS Row.

Shape Neck

Work 18 (20, 22, 25, 27) sts in patt, join new ball of yarn and BO 27 sts, work rem sts in patt.
   Work 3 rows even.
Next row: (RS; dec row) Left shoulder: work in patt to last 4 sts, ssk, k2; right shoulder: k2, k2tog, work in patt to end—1 st dec'd each shoulder.
Rep dec row every 4th row 3 (3, 3, 4, 4) times—14 (16, 18, 20, 22) sts rem.
   Work even in patt as for Back to shoulder shaping. Shape shoulders as for back.

**Left Sleeve
Lace Pattern**

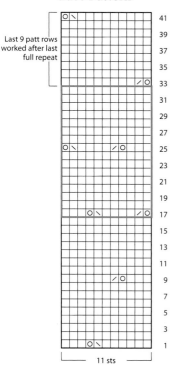

Last 9 patt rows
worked after last
full repeat

41
39
37
35
33
31
29
27
25
23
21
19
17
15
13
11
9
7
5
3
1

⌐ 11 sts ⌐

**Right Cable
Pattern**

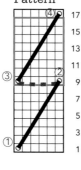

17
15
13
11
9
7
5
3
1

**Left Cable
Pattern**

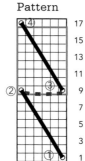

17
15
13
11
9
7
5
3
1

**Right Sleeve & Center
Cable Pattern**

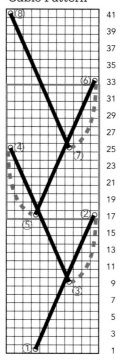

41
39
37
35
33
31
29
27
25
23
21
19
17
15
13
11
9
7
5
3
1

**Left Sleeve
Cable Pattern**

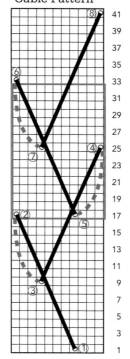

41
39
37
35
33
31
29
27
25
23
21
19
17
15
13
11
9
7
5
3
1

Mock Cable Pattern

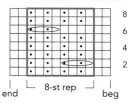

8
6
4
2

⌐ 8-st rep ⌐
end   beg

☐ k on RS; p on WS

• p on RS; k on WS

⬭ yo, [k1, p1] twice, sl yo

☐ pattern repeat box

━━━ I-cord across RS

▪ ▪ ▪ I-cord across WS

① Thread cords following
     numerical order

SLEEVES

Note: Work Right Sleeve & Center Lace
Patt for right sleeve and Left Sleeve Lace
Patt for left sleeve.

With MC and cir needle, CO 45 sts.
Set-up row: (WS) P17, pm, p11, pm, p17.
Row 1: K17, work Center Lace Patt, k17.
Work in patt as established, working
Center Lace Patt over center 11 sts and St
st at beg and end of row, for 1 row.
Next row: (RS; inc row) K2, M1, work in
patt to last 2 sts, M1, k2—2 sts inc'd.
Rep inc row every 4th rows 0 (0, 0, 6, 15)
times, every 6th row 0 (5, 16, 12, 6) times,
every 8th row 6 (18, 0, 0, 0) times, and
every 10th row 5 (0, 0, 0, 0) times—67 (71,
77, 81, 87) sts.

Work even in patt until piece measures
14" (35.5 cm), ending after a WS row.

Shape Cap
BO 6 (7, 7, 8, 8) sts at beg of next 2
rows—55 (57, 63, 65, 71) sts rem.
Next row: (RS; dec row) K2, k2tog, work
in patt to last 4 sts, ssk, k2—2 sts dec'd.
Rep dec row every RS row 13 (13, 13, 14,
14) more times—27 (29, 35, 35, 41)
sts rem.

SIZES 39½", 42", AND 44½"
Next row: (WS; dec row) P2, ssp, work to
last 4 sts, p2tog, p2—2 sts dec'd.
Rep last 2 rows (RS and WS dec rows) 1 (1,
2) more time(s)—29 (29, 31) sts rem.

BO 3 sts at beg of next 4 (2, 2, 2, 2) rows, then BO 4 sts at beg of next 0 (2, 2, 2, 2) rows—15 (15, 15, 15, 17) sts rem.

At the same time, when piece measures 3¼ (3¼, 3¾, 4, 4½)" (8.5 [8.5, 9.5, 10, 11.5] cm) from start of Cap shaping, end Lace Patt with a complete rep. Cont cap shaping and work last 9 rows of patt chart.

BO rem sts.

FINISHING

Block pieces to measurements.

I-cord

With CC and dpns, CO 3 sts. Work 3-st I-cord (see Glossary) for 4" (10 cm). BO and cut yarn, leaving a 6" (15 cm) tail.

Make four 54" (137 cm) 3-st I-cords for side "cables" of Front and Back.

Make two 80" (203 cm) 3-st I-cords for Sleeves.

Make one 70" (178 cm) 3-st I-cord for Front Center Lace Patt for center "cable."

Make one 135" (343 cm) 3-st I-cord for Back Center Lace Patt for center "cable."

Using Cable charts as guides and beg with CO ends, thread respective I-cords through eyelets. (If I-cords are too long, remove BO and shorten as needed, then BO again.) When you are satisfied with placement, secure ends of I-cords to WS of sweater.

With MC threaded on a tapestry needle, sew shoulder seams. Sew in sleeves. Sew underarm and side seams.

Hood

With MC, cir needle, and RS facing, pick up and knit (see Glossary) 20 (20, 20, 23, 23) sts evenly along Right Front Neck

edge, 48 sts along straight portion of right edge of Back Hood, 72 (72, 72, 74, 74) sts along shaped top of Back Hood, 48 sts evenly along straight portion of left edge of Back Hood, and 20 (20, 20, 23, 23) sts along Left Front Neck edge—208 (208, 208, 216, 216) sts.

Work Mock Cable patt and *at the same time* inc on RS as foll:

Next row: (RS; inc row) K2, M1, work in patt to last 2 sts, M1, k2—2 sts inc'd. Rep inc row every 4th row, working inc sts into rib patt and working yo and sl yo when enough sts become available 7 more times—224 (224, 224, 232, 232) sts. Work even in patt until piece measures 5" (12.5 cm) from pick-up row, ending after a WS row. BO all sts firmly in patt.

Bottom Edging

With MC, cir needles, and RS facing, pick up and knit 1 st in each st along CO edge of Front and Back—174 (186, 198, 210, 222) sts. Join for working in the rnd.

With MC and one dpn, work next 3 sts from cir needle as foll: [K3, turn, p3, turn] 6 times; leave sts on dpn. Rep with CC and second dpn.

*Lift dpn holding MC sts over second and hold behind next 3 sts on cir needle. [K1 st from cir needle tog with 1 st from dpn] 3 times, turn, p3 with dpn, [k3, turn, p3, turn] 5 times; leave sts on dpn. Rep with CC.

Rep from * until no sts rem on cir needle.

With MC threaded on a tapestry needle, use Kitchener st (see Glossary) to graft sts from first dpn to base of original MC sts. Rep with CC, second dpn, and original MC sts.

Sleeve Edging

With MC, 3 dpns, and RS facing, pick up and knit 42 sts evenly along bottom of sleeve. Work as for Bottom Edging.

Weave in ends.

cable
integration

By now, you have skills to create most any type of cable you
desire. How will you use it? Do you want to modify a pattern to
include a cable, swap one cable for another, or design a cabled
piece of your very own? In addition to understanding how
cables work and how they affect knitted fabric, there are
several design principles that will put you on the road to cable-
design success.

SIZE MATTERS

One important factor in choosing a cable is the size of the project. Keeping the scale of the cables to the scale of the project is generally a good idea. For a large piece such as an afghan, you may decide to use larger cable patterns. For a medium-sized piece such as a stole or a sweater, choose cables in a medium size. A scarf, which is only a few inches wide, requires smaller cables so that you can fit a few within the confines of its size. (That's not to say that a scarf can't be comprised of a single large cable or that an afghan can't be made up of lots of small cables, tedious though it may be.) It's easy to begin with a small cable and expand it to fit your needs.

There are three ways to enlarge a cable:

* Use big yarns and large needles (**Figs. 1a and 1b**). Cables in a sock yarn and size 2 needles are far smaller than cables in a chunky yarn and size 10 needles.

* Work more stitches in each set (**Figs. 2a and 2b**). Instead of a 4-stitch rope cable (2 over 2 stitches, crossed every fourth row with 3 plain rows between crossings), make it a 12-stitch rope (6 over 6 stitches, crossed every twelfth row with 11 plain rows between crossings).

* Use more repeats of the cable. Instead of a single braid, add multiple braids (see page 17 for ways to add cables

together). Instead of just four mirror-image braids, work six or eight.

Use these ideas to make a cable to any size you like—a small, subtle twist; a complex labyrinth; a simple but oversized rope cable; any cable you can dream up.

Fig. 1a   Fig. 1b

Fig. 1: Two 2/2 left ropes, one worked in thicker yarn on larger needles, the other in thinner yarn on smaller needles.

Fig. 2a   Fig. 2b

Fig. 2: A 2/2 left cross and a 6/6 left cross.

Fig. 3: Textured intarsia cables.

Fig. 4: Textured stranded-colorwork cables.

Fig. 5: Textured pinstripe cables.

Fig. 6: Colorized traveling-stitch cables.

Fig. 7: Lace wide-rib reversible cables.

COMBINING CABLES

There are infinite possible combinations of cables, too many for one book. In addition to each of the methods we've explored in depth, you can combine more than one technique to create interesting hybrids and variations. With these ideas, use your creativity to invent your own original cable patterns combinations.

Color cable techniques can be especially exciting when combined with textured and traveling stitches. For instance, pair intarsia cables with textured cables to produce garter stitch of one color crossed over stockinette of another color (Fig. 3).

Work stranded-colorwork cables in garter stitch for texture (Fig. 4). Add texture to pinstripe cables, a variation on corrugated ribbing in classic stranded colorwork: work the knit stitches in one color and the purl stitches in another color (Fig. 5). Work a traveling stitch pattern with the background in one color and the traveling stitches in another (Fig. 6). Begin with reversible wide rib cables, and texturize them with lace wales (Fig. 7).

When you understand how each of the cable techniques works by itself, practice pairing two or more of your favorites to create an exciting new look.

DESIGNING CABLED GARMENTS

When I design cabled projects from scratch, I measure the width of each cable used and the gauge of my background or "filler stitch." I lay out the cables on square graph paper, with each square representing one inch. Then I figure out how many filler or separator stitches are needed in each section between the cables to produce the desired width in their respective gauge (Fig. 8).

One good "cheat" is to make several photocopies of (or scan and print) each of your swatches of cables and filler stitches. Physically cut and paste them together to try out different options. Not only can you see how the different patterns look together, you also have many sheets of

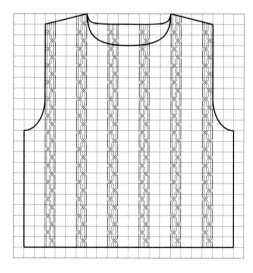

Fig. 8: Laying down cables on square graph paper.

Fig. 9: Half-drop cable with no separator stitches.

Fig. 10: Half-drop cable with 4 purl separator stitches.

paper representing a life-sized project. You can see how big the pieces and patterns will be. You can even hold the paper up to yourself to see how it would look as a garment on you or place it on the bed to see how it looks as an afghan. I use my scanner and printer for a full-color version.

Cables don't have to fill the whole piece. It's typical for any cable to have purl "filler" stitches on each side to accentuate the cable. Other possible filler stitches include moss, seed, double moss, or even garter. You can widen a piece with more filler stitches between the cables. Cables look more complex when mashed up together, as we saw in the repeats of a single braid on page 17. With filler stitches between cables, it is far easier to make out the braid, rather than looking at a sea of fabric that's nothing but cables. Compare a half-drop rope with no separator stitches (**Fig. 9**)

to a half-drop rope with purl separator stitches (**Fig. 10**).

Since cables pull in a fabric and thicken it, filler stitches not only lighten up a piece and make it less heavy and dense, they also reduce "knittus interruptus." Cables interrupt the flow of knitting; you have to stop and pick up a cable needle or rearrange the order of the stitches. With fewer cables in a piece, there's less interruption.

When incorporating cables into any knitted sweater or pillow or handbag design, remember that cables create a denser and narrower piece. The gauge of the cable stitches will be different than that of stockinette stitch, for instance. Compensate accordingly—if you modify a pattern designed entirely in stockinette stitch to add a cable, some stitches must be added to compensate for the width drawn in. How many you add depends on the particular cable pattern. Measure

the width of the cable in your sample swatch (and you do swatch, right?). Let's say a 6-stitch braid measures one inch wide. Compare that measurement with the gauge given in the directions for the project, in stockinette or the pattern stitch gauge; we'll use 4 stitches per inch in our example. Wherever you want to insert a cable, you will need 6 stitches over that inch instead of 4 stitches.

GO FORTH AND CABLE!

Well, there you have it—more kinds of cables than you ever thought possible, plus the skills to use them in any way you can imagine. Whether you're planning to dream up cabled garments from scratch or just understand how they work in an already-written pattern, use the techniques you've learned to create rich, exciting knits.

abbreviations

beg(s)	begin(s); beginning		**sl**	slip
BO	bind off		**sl st**	slip st (slip 1 stitch purlwise unless otherwise indicated)
CC	contrasting color		**ssk**	slip 2 stitches knitwise, one at a time, from the left needle to right needle, insert left needle tip through both front loops and knit together from this position (1 stitch decrease)
cm	centimeter(s)			
cn	cable needle			
CO	cast on			
cont	continue(s); continuing			
dec(s)	decrease(s); decreasing		**ssp**	slip 2 stitches purlwise, one at a time, from the left needle to right needle, insert left needle tip through both front loops and purl together from this position (1 stitch decrease)
dpn(s)	double-pointed needle(s)			
foll	follow(s); following			
g	gram(s)			
inc(s)	increase(s); increasing			
k	knit		**st(s)**	stitch(es)
k1f&b	knit into the front and back of same stitch		**St st**	stockinette stitch
			tbl	through back loop
k2tog	knit two stitches together		**tog**	together
kwise	knitwise, as if to knit		**WS**	wrong side
m	marker(s)		**wyb**	with yarn in back
MC	main color		**wyf**	with yarn in front
mm	millimeter(s)		**yd**	yard(s)
M1	make one (increase)		**yo(s)**	yarnover(s)
p	purl		*	repeat starting point
p1f&b	purl into front and back of same stitch		* *	repeat all instructions between asterisks
patt(s)	pattern(s)		( )	alternate measurements and/or instructions
psso	pass slipped stitch over			
p2sso	pass two slipped stitches over		[ ]	work instructions as a group a specified number of times
pwise	purlwise, as if to purl			
rem	remain(s); remaining			
rep	repeat(s); repeating			
rev St st	reverse stockinette stitch			
rnd(s)	round(s)			
RS	right side			

glossary

BIND-OFFS

3-Needle Bind-off
Place the stitches to be joined onto two separate needles and hold the needles parallel so that the right sides of knitting face together. Insert a third needle into the first stitch on each of two needles **(Figure 1)** and knit them together as one stitch **(Figure 2)**, *knit the next stitch on each needle the same way, then use the left needle tip to lift the first stitch over the second and off the needle **(Figure 3)**. Repeat from * until no stitches remain on first two needles. Cut yarn and pull tail through last stitch to secure.

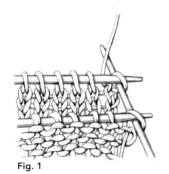

Fig. 1

Fig. 2

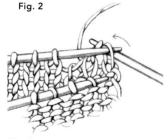

Fig. 3

BLOCKING

Steam Blocking
Pin the pieces to be blocked to a blocking surface. Hold an iron set on the steam setting ½" (1.3 cm) above the knitted surface and direct the steam over the entire surface (except ribbing). You can get similar results by lapping wet cheesecloth on top of the knitted surface and touching it lightly with a dry iron. Lift and set down the iron gently; do not use a pushing motion.

CAST-ONS

Backward-Loop Cast-on
*Loop working yarn and place it on needle backward so that it doesn't unwind. Repeat from *.

Cable Cast-on
If there are no stitches on the needles, make a slipknot of working yarn and place it on the needle, then use the knitted method (see next page) to cast-on one more stitch—2 stitches on needle. Hold needle with working yarn in your left hand with the wrong side of the work facing you. *Insert right needle between the first 2 stitches on left needle **(Figure 1)**, wrap yarn around needle as if to knit, draw yarn through **(Figure 2)**, and place new loop on left needle **(Figure 3)** to form a new stitch. Repeat from * for the desired number of stitches, always working between the first 2 stitches on the left needle.

Fig. 1

Fig. 2

Fig. 3

Chain-Edge Cast-on

Place a slipknot on a crochet hook. Hold the needle and yarn in your left hand with the yarn under the needle. Place hook over needle, wrap yarn around hook, and pull the loop through the slipknot (**Figure 1**). *Bring yarn to back under needle, wrap yarn around hook, and pull it through loop on hook (**Figure 2**). Repeat from * until there is one less than the desired number of stitches. Bring the yarn to the back and slip the remaining loop from the hook onto the needle.

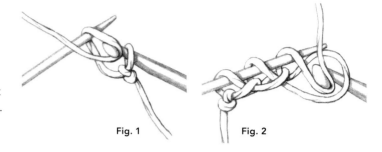

Fig. 1   Fig. 2

Circular Cast-on

This method for casting on for a circle in the round is invisible. With the yarn tail held in your left hand, make a loop over your fingers and hold the working yarn between your thumb and index finger (**Figure 1**). *Insert the needle through the middle of the loop, wrap the working yarn around it, and draw it back through. Yarn over (**Figure 2**). Rep from * for desired number of stitches (**Figure 3**). This method produces an odd number of stitches (**Figure 4**). Arrange stitches on needles and pull tail to snug the circle. For an even number of stitches, yarnover before working the first stitch in the round.

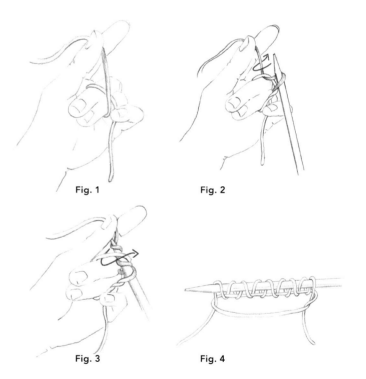

Fig. 1   Fig. 2

Fig. 3   Fig. 4

160

Knitted Cast-on

Make a slipknot of working yarn and place it on the left needle if there are no stitches already there. *Use the right needle to knit the first stitch (or slipknot) on left needle **(Figure 1)** and place new loop onto left needle to form a new stitch **(Figure 2)**. Repeat from * for the desired number of stitches, always working into the last stitch made.

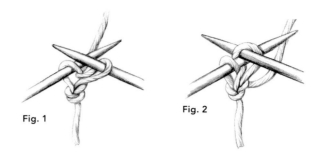

Fig. 1   Fig. 2

Long-tail (Continental) Cast-on

Leaving a long tail (about ½" [1.3 cm] for each stitch to be cast on), make a slipknot and place on right needle. Place thumb and index finger of your left hand between the yarn ends so that working yarn is around your index finger and tail end is around your thumb and secure the yarn ends with your other fingers. Hold your palm upward, making a V of yarn **(Figure 1)**. *Bring needle up through loop on thumb **(Figure 2)**, catch first strand around index finger, and go back down through loop on thumb **(Figure 3)**. Drop loop off thumb and, placing thumb back in V configuration, tighten resulting stitch on needle **(Figure 4)**. Repeat from * for the desired number of stitches.

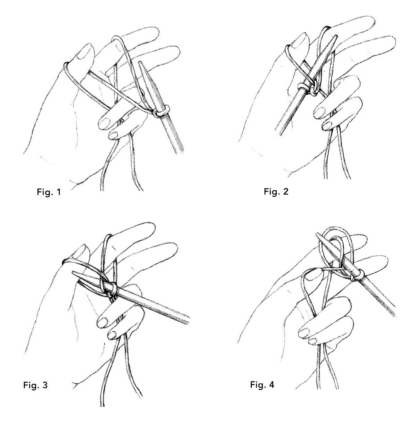

Fig. 1   Fig. 2

Fig. 3   Fig. 4

CROCHET

Crochet Chain (ch)

Make a slipknot and place it on crochet hook if there isn't a loop already on the hook. *Yarn over hook and draw through loop on hook. Repeat from * for the desired number of stitches. To fasten off, cut yarn and draw end through last loop formed.

Single Crochet (sc)

*Insert hook into the second chain from the hook (or the next stitch), yarn over hook and draw through a loop, yarn over hook **(Figure 1)**, and draw it through both loops on hook **(Figure 2)**. Repeat from * for the desired number of stitches.

Fig. 1   Fig. 2

Slip-Stitch Crochet (sl st)

*Insert hook into stitch, yarn over hook and draw a loop through both the stitch and the loop already on hook. Repeat from * for the desired number of stitches.

DECREASES

Centered Double Decrease (sl 2, k1, p2sso)

Slip 2 stitches together knitwise **(Figure 1)**, knit the next stitch **(Figure 2)**, then pass the slipped stitches over the knitted stitch **(Figure 3)**.

Fig. 1

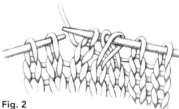

Fig. 2

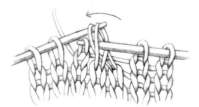

Fig. 3

Left-Slant Double Decrease (sl 1, k2tog, psso)

Slip 1 stitch knitwise to right needle, knit the next 2 stitches together (**Figure 1**), then use the tip of the left needle to lift the slipped stitch up and over the knitted stitches (**Figure 2**), then off the needle.

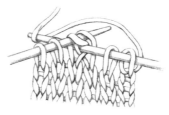

Fig. 1

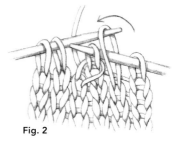

Fig. 2

Slip 1, Knit 1, Pass Slipped Stitch Over (sl 1, k1, psso)

Slip 1 stitch knitwise, knit the next stitch (**Figure 1**), then use the left needle tip to lift the slipped stitch over the knitted stitch and off the needle (**Figure 2**).

Fig. 1

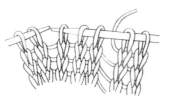

Fig. 2

Slip, Slip, Slip, Knit (sssk)

Slip 3 stitches individually knitwise (**Figure 1**), insert left needle tip into the front of these 3 slipped stitches, and use the right needle to knit them together through their back loops (**Figure 2**).

Fig. 1

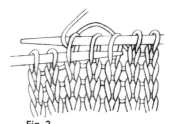

Fig. 2

Slip, Slip, Purl (ssp)

Holding yarn in front, slip 2 stitches individually knitwise (**Figure 1**), then slip these 2 stitches back onto left needle (they will be turned on the needle) and purl them together through their back loops (**Figure 2**).

Fig. 1

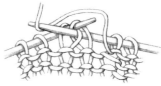

Fig. 2

GRAFTING

Kitchener Stitch

Arrange stitches on two needles so that there is the same number of stitches on each needle. Hold the needles parallel to each other with wrong sides of the knitting together. Allowing about ½" (1.3 cm) per stitch to be grafted, thread matching yarn on a tapestry needle. Work from right to left as follows:

Step 1. Bring tapestry needle through the first stitch on the front needle as if to purl and leave the stitch on the needle (**Figure 1**).

Step 2. Bring tapestry needle through the first stitch on the back needle as if to knit and leave that stitch on the needle (**Figure 2**).

Step 3. Bring tapestry needle through the first front stitch as if to knit and slip this stitch off the needle, then bring tapestry needle through the next front stitch as if to purl and leave this stitch on the needle (**Figure 3**).

Step 4. Bring tapestry needle through the first back stitch as if to purl and slip this stitch off the needle, then bring tapestry needle through the next back stitch as if to knit and leave this stitch on the needle (**Figure 4**).

Repeat Steps 3 and 4 until 1 stitch remains on each needle, adjusting the tension to match the rest of the knitting as you go. To finish, bring tapestry needle through the front stitch as if to knit and slip this stitch off the needle, then bring tapestry needle through the back stitch as if to purl and slip this stitch off the needle.

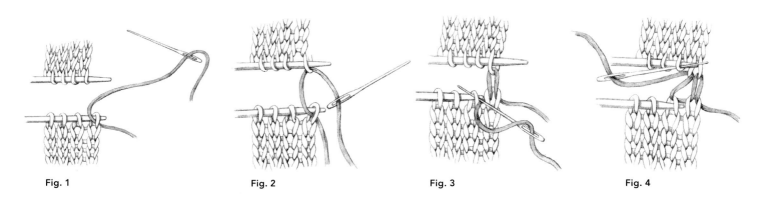

Fig. 1   Fig. 2   Fig. 3   Fig. 4

I-CORD (also called Knit-Cord)

Using two double-pointed needles, cast on the desired number of stitches (usually 3 to 4). *Without turning the needle, slide stitches to other end of needle, pull the yarn around the back, and knit the stitches as usual. Repeat from * for desired length.

INCREASES

Bar Increase (k1f&b)

Knit into a stitch but leave it on the left needle **(Figure 1)**, then knit through the back loop of the same stitch **(Figure 2)** and slip the original stitch off the needle **(Figure 3)**.

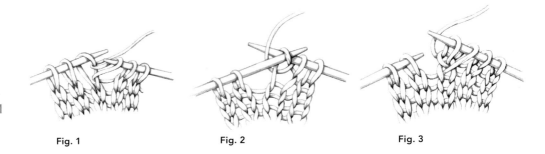

Fig. 1   Fig. 2   Fig. 3

Lifted Increase—Left Slant

Insert left needle tip into the back of the stitch below the stitch just knitted **(Figure 1)**, then knit this stitch **(Figure 2)**.

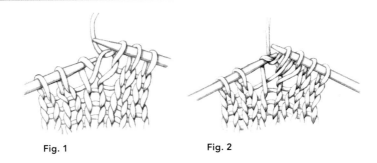

Fig. 1   Fig. 2

Lifted Increase—Right Slant

Note: If no slant direction is specified, use the right slant.

Knit into the back of the stitch (in the "purl bump") in the row directly below the stitch on the needle **(Figure 1)**, then knit the stitch on the needle **(Figure 2)** and slip the original stitch off the needle.

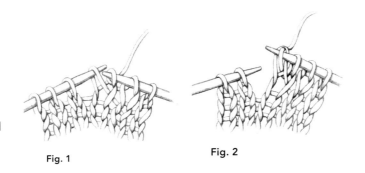

Fig. 1   Fig. 2

Make One—Left Slant (M1L)

Note: Use the left slant if no direction of slant is specified.

With left needle tip, lift the strand between the last knitted stitch and the first stitch on the left needle from front to back **(Figure 1)**, then knit the lifted loop through the back **(Figure 2)**.

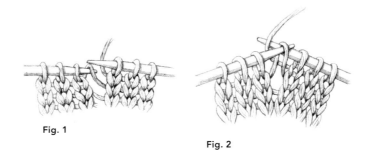

Fig. 1   Fig. 2

Make One Purlwise (M1 pwise)

With left needle tip, lift the strand between the needles from back to front (**Figure 1**), then purl the lifted loop through the front (**Figure 2**).

Fig. 1

Fig. 2

Make One—Right Slant (M1R)

With left needle tip, lift the strand between the needles from back to front (**Figure 1**). Knit the lifted loop through the front (**Figure 2**).

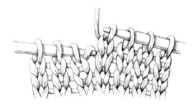

Fig. 1

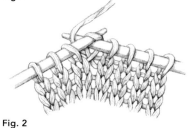

Fig. 2

Yarnovers

BACKWARD YARNOVER

Bring the yarn to the back under the needle, then over the top to the front so that the leading leg of the loop is at the back of the needle.

YARNOVER BETWEEN 2 KNIT STITCHES

Wrap the working yarn around the needle from front to back and in position to knit the next stitch.

YARNOVER AFTER A KNIT BEFORE A PURL

Wrap the working yarn around the needle from front to back, then under the needle to the front again in position to purl the next stitch.

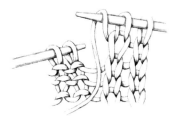

YARNOVER AFTER PURL BEFORE KNIT

Wrap the working yarn around the needle from front to back and in position to knit the next stitch.

YARNOVER BETWEEN 2 PURL STS

Wrap the working yarn around the needle from front to back, then under the needle to the front in position to purl the next stitch.

KNIT STITCH

Knit into the Row Below

Work to the stitch to be worked below (**Figure 1**). Insert tip of right needle into stitch below next stitch on left needle, work it as a knit stitch, and drop the stitch from the left needle (**Figure 2**). The stitch is "caught" and will not ravel.

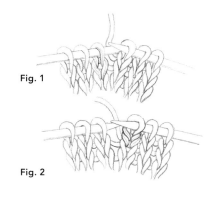

Fig. 1

Fig. 2

Knit Through Back Loop (tbl)

Insert right needle through the loop on the back of the left needle from front to back, wrap the yarn around the needle, and pull a loop through while slipping the stitch off the left needle. This is similar to a regular knit stitch but is worked into the back loop of the stitch instead of the front.

PICK UP AND KNIT

Pick Up and Knit Along CO or BO Edge

With right side facing and working from right to left, insert the tip of the needle into the center of the stitch below the bind-off or cast-on edge (**Figure 1**), wrap yarn around needle, and pull through a loop (**Figure 2**). Pick up one stitch for every existing stitch.

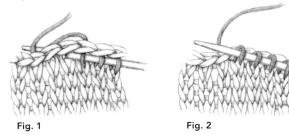

Fig. 1

Fig. 2

Pick Up and Knit Along Shaped Edge

With right side facing and working from right to left, insert tip of needle between last and second-to-last stitches, wrap yarn around needle, and pull through a loop. Pick up and knit about 3 stitches for every 4 rows, adjusting as necessary so that picked-up edge lays flat.

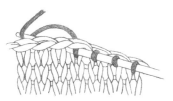

Pick Up and Purl

With wrong side of work facing and working from right to left, *insert needle tip under selvedge stitch from the far side to the near side, wrap yarn around needle (**Figure 1**), and pull a loop through (**Figure 2**). Repeat from * for desired number of stitches.

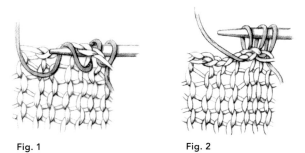

Fig. 1

Fig. 2

PURL STITCH

Purl Into the Row Below

Work to the stitch to be worked below **(Figure 1)**. Insert tip of right needle into stitch below next stitch on left needle, work it as a purl stitch, and drop the stitch from the left needle **(Figure 2)**. The stitch is "caught" and will not ravel.

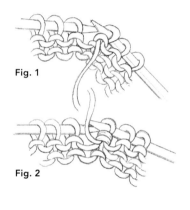

Fig. 1

Fig. 2

Purl Through Back Loop

Insert right needle through the loop of the back of the left needle from back to front, wrap the yarn around the needle, and pull a loop through while slipping the stitch off the left needle. This is similar to a regular purl stitch, but is worked into the back loop of the stitch instead of the front.

SEAMS

Invisible Horizontal Seam

Working with the bound-off edges opposite each other, right sides of the knitting facing you, and working into the stitches just below the bound-off edges, bring threaded tapestry needle out at the center of the first stitch (i.e., go under half of the first stitch) on one side of the seam, then bring needle in and out under the first whole stitch on the other side **(Figure 1)**. *Bring needle into the center of the same stitch it came out of before, then out in the center of the adjacent stitch **(Figure 2)**. Bring needle in and out under the next whole stitch on the other side **(Figure 3)**. Repeat from *, ending with a half-stitch on the first side.

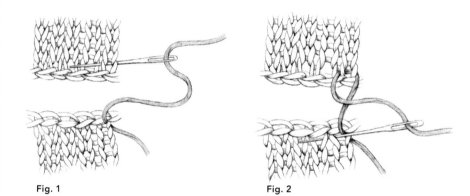

Fig. 1

Fig. 2

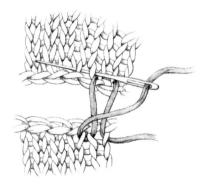

Fig. 3

Invisible Vertical to Horizontal Seam

With yarn threaded on a tapestry needle, pick up one bar between the first 2 stitches along the vertical edge (**Figure 1**), then pick up 1 complete stitch along the horizontal edge (**Figure 2**). *Pick up the next one or two bars on the first piece, then the next whole stitch on the other piece (**Figure 3**). Repeat from *, ending by picking up one bar on the vertical edge.

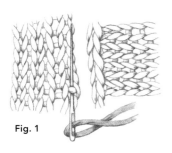

Fig. 1

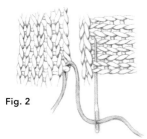

Fig. 2

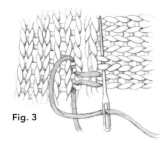

Fig. 3

Invisible Vertical Seam or Mattress Stitch

Place the pieces to be seamed on a table, right sides facing up. Begin at the lower edge and work upward as follows:

Insert threaded needle under one bar between the 2 edge stitches on one piece, then under the corresponding bar plus the bar above it on the other piece (**Figure 1**). *Pick up the next two bars on the first piece (**Figure 2**), then the next two bars on the other (**Figure 3**). Repeat from *, ending by picking up the last bar or pair of bars on the first piece.

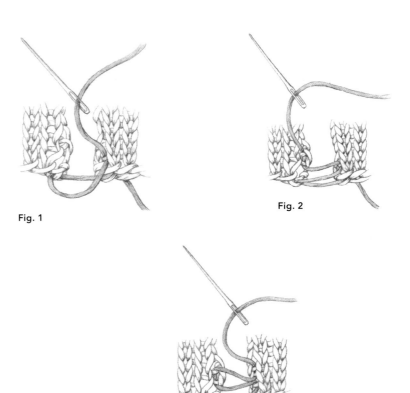

Fig. 1

Fig. 2

Fig. 3

SHORT-ROWS

Short-Rows (Knit Side)
Work to turning point, slip next stitch purlwise (**Figure 1**), bring the yarn to the front, then slip the same stitch back to the left needle (**Figure 2**), turn the work around and bring the yarn in position for the next stitch—1 stitch has been wrapped and the yarn is correctly positioned to work the next stitch. When you come to a wrapped stitch on a subsequent row, hide the wrap by working it together with the wrapped stitch as follows: Insert right needle tip under the wrap (from the front if wrapped stitch is a knit stitch; from the back if wrapped stitch is a purl stitch; **Figure 3**), then into the stitch on the needle, and work the stitch and its wrap together as a single stitch.

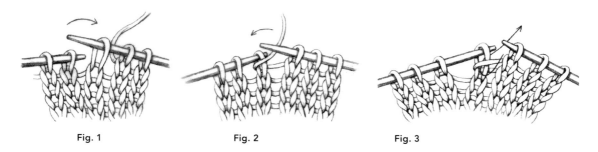

Fig. 1   Fig. 2   Fig. 3

Short-Rows (Purl Side)
Work to the turning point, slip the next stitch purlwise to the right needle, bring the yarn to the back of the work (**Figure 1**), return the slipped stitch to the left needle, bring the yarn to the front between the needles (**Figure 2**), and turn the work so that the knit side is facing—1 stitch has been wrapped and the yarn is correctly positioned to knit the next stitch. To hide the wrap on a subsequent purl row, work to the wrapped stitch, use the tip of the right needle to pick up the wrap from the back, place it on the left needle (**Figure 3**), then purl it together with the wrapped stitch.

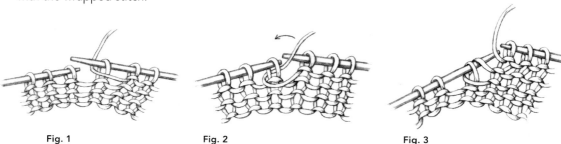

Fig. 1   Fig. 2   Fig. 3

SPLICING

Split Splice

To splice together two balls of yarn, untwist an inch or two from the end of each ball (**Figure 1**), overlap the raveled ends (**Figure 2**), moisten them with water (saliva works well and is always available, though not always the most polite). Place the overlapped loose fibers in one palm and use your other palm to vigorously rub the two ends together (**Figure 3**). The moisture and friction will cause the two yarn ends to felt together. (*Note:* This method only works for yarns that are predominantly wool.)

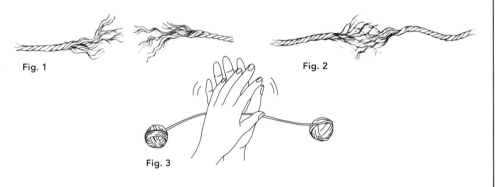

Fig. 1   Fig. 2

Fig. 3

Russian Join

Make sure to leave a 6" (15 cm) tail of old yarn to work the Russian join. With the tail of the old yarn threaded on a needle (sharper than a tapestry needle if possible), pass the needle through the old yarn several times to anchor (**Figure 1**). Pull the tail through but leave an opening to pass the new yarn through. With the new yarn threaded on a tapestry needle, pass through the opening left by the old yarn, then pass the needle back and forth through the new yarn (**Figure 2**). Pull both tails to tighten the join (**Figure 3**) until it is nearly invisible. Trim loose ends if needed.

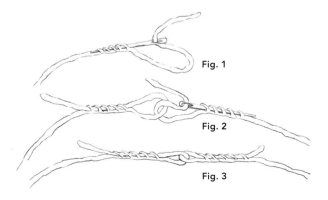

Fig. 1

Fig. 2

Fig. 3

ZIPPER

With right side facing and zipper closed, pin zipper to the knitted pieces so edges cover the zipper teeth. With contrasting thread and right side facing, baste zipper in place close to teeth (**Figure 1**). Turn work over and with matching sewing thread and needle, stitch outer edges of zipper to wrong side of knitting (**Figure 2**), being careful to follow a single column of stitches in the knitting to keep zipper straight. Turn work back to right side facing, wand with matching sewing thread, sew knitted fabric close to teeth (**Figure 3**). Remove basting.

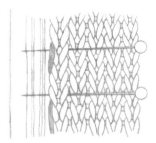

Fig. 1

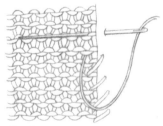

Fig. 2

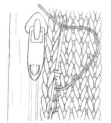

Fig. 3

further reading

Power Cables is the result of many years designing
with cables and teaching cable techniques. It has been over
twenty years since I developed my method for knitting
reversible ribbed cables, and since I have published articles
and designs with cables in a number of magazines, books,
and other publications. Techniques of machine knitting have
been a particular source of inspiration, and I have designed a
number of patterns for cabled machine knits as well. If you're
interested in exploring these techniques further or tracing
their development, check out one of the resources below.

Brown Sheep Yarn Company.
   Color cable (real and phony) yoked
   sweater (cable pattern shown page 135)

Chin, Lily M. *The Urban Knitter.*
   New York: Berkeley Books, 2002.
   "A Slew of Socks," reversible cable socks
   (cable shown in Stitch File, page 32)

Family Circle Easy Knitting, 2006.
   Phony two-color cable belt (technique
   shown in Two-Colored Handbag, pages
   136–141)

Fiber Trends.
   "Dancing Flames," textured, reversibly
   cabled scarf/stole/afghan (cable shown
   in Stitch File, page 70)

Fiber Trends.
   "Pocketed Stoles and Scarves," wide-
   rib wales baby cables (cable shown in
   Stitch File, page 32)

Fiber Trends.
   "Reversibly Cabled, Textured Afghan,"
   panels of ribbed rope, basketweave
   cables, and textured mirrored braids

Kooler, Donna. *Encyclopedia of Knitting.*
   Little Rock, Arkansas: Leisure Arts, 2004.
   "Reversible Wrap" ribbed braid,
   basketweave, and textured OXO (shown
   in Stitch File, page 71)

Knitty Gritty season 6.
   "Nine-Block Baby Blanket," reversible blanket with a block of reversible
   bi-colored rib (shown in Stitch File,
   page 110) and ribbed repeated braids
   (nonreversible version shown in Stitch
   File, top of page 17)

Knitter's #17 (Winter 1989; mohair issue).
"On Design" column: Original "ribbles" article and afghan pattern with ribbed "shadow diamonds" (nonreversible version shown in Stitch File, page 20) and ribbed spiral cables (nonreversible version shown in Stitch File, page 18)

Knitter's #36 (Fall 1994; Africa issue).
"Mali Mudcloth" pinstriped cable pattern (shown as Figure 7 on page 109)

Knitter's #38 (Spring 1995; ribs issue).
Cabled reversible two-color stole (shown as Figure 9 on page 111)

Knitter's #53 (Winter 1998; North Country issue).
"Hank Aran" texturally cabled pattern such as that on page 72.

Knitter's #64 (Fall 2001; cables issue).
Raised wale cables with a different pattern on each side (technique demonstrated in Chapter 7), and "Mohair Cables," woman's sweater with OXO cable (non-reversible version shown in Stitch File, page 71)

Machine Knit America, volume 2, number 5 (March/April 1993).
"Reversibly Cabled Stole," wide-rib reversible cables (shown in Chapter 2) in "Traveling Couple" cables (shown in Figures 23–26, page 23)

Machine Knit America, volume 2, number 6 (May/June 1993).
"Reversibly Cabled Jacket," raised wale cables (shown in Chapter 7) in "Traveling Couple" cables (shown in Figures 23–26, page 23)

Machine Knit America, volume 3, number 1 (July/August 1993).
"Reversibly Cabled Sweater," ribbed cables (shown in Chapter 3) in "Traveling Couple" cables (shown in Figures 23–26, page 23)

Machine Knit America, volume 3, number 3 (November/December 1993).
Pinstriped cables (shown in Figure 4, page 108)

Orphan Foundation of America (orphan.org).
Reversible mock cable scarf (shown in hood of "Three-Fakes Hoodie," pages 147–153)

Studio by White Design, May/June 1992.
Saddle Shouldered Tunic with pinstripe cables (translated for handknitting as "Pinstriped Cable Pullover," pages 112–117)

Vogue Knitting, Spring/Summer 1990.
"Dancing Flames pullover" (cover), textured cable pattern (nonreversible version shown in Stitch File, page 70)

Vogue Knitting, Fall 1990.
"Aran Ribbles" scarf (cover), ribbed reversible cables (technique shown in Chapter 3)

Vogue Knitting, Winter 1999/2000; reprinted in the book *Vogue Knitting American Collection.*
"Reversible Cabled-Rib Shawl," of ribbed sand cables (shown in Stitch File, page 70)

Vogue Knitting, Fall 2005.
Phony two-color cable bag strap (technique shown in Two-Colored Handbag, pages 136–141)

Vogue Knitting on the Go: Shawls.
"Reversible Cable Shawl," ribbed repeating braids (nonreversible version shown in Stitch File, bottom of page 17)

yarn suppliers

Berroco Inc.
14 Elmdale Rd.
PO Box 367
Uxbridge, MA 01569-0367
(508) 278-2527
berroco.com

Cascade Yarns
1224 Andover Park E.
Tukwila, WA 98188
(800) 548-1048
cascadeyarns.com

Classic Elite Yarns
122 Western Ave.
Lowell, MA 01851-1434
(978) 453-2837
classiceliteyarns.com

Crystal Palace Yarns
160 23rd Ave.
Richmond, CA 94804
(510) 237-9988
straw.com

Karabella Yarns
1201 Broadway
New York, NY 10001
(212) 684-2665
karabellayarns.com

Kraemer Yarns
PO Box 72
Nazareth, PA 18064-0072
(610) 759-4030
kraemeryarns.com

Louet Sales
808 Commerce Park Dr.
Ogdensburg, NY 13669
(800) 897-6444
louet.com

Mission Falls
5333 Casgrain Ave.
Ste. 1204
Montreal, QC
Canada H2T 1X3
(877) 244-1204
missionfalls.com

Plymouth Yarns
500 Lafayette St.
Bristol, PA 19007
(215) 788-0459
plymouthyarn.com

Reynolds Yarns/JCA Inc.
35 Scales Ln.
Townsend, MA 01469
(800) 225-6340
jcacrafts.com

Skacel Collection Inc.
PO Box 88110
Seattle, WA 98138-2110
(253) 854-2710
skacelknitting.com

Tahki Stacy Charles Inc.
70-30 80th St. Bldg. 36
Ridgewood, NY 11385
(800) 338-YARN
tahkistacycharles.com

Trendsetter Yarns/ Mondial
16745 Saticoy St.
Ste. 101
VanNuys, CA 91406
(800) 446-2425
trendsetteryarns.com

index

stitch index